DESIGN & THE DECORATIVE ARTS

TUDOR AND STUART BRITAIN 1500-1714

DESIGN & THE DECORATIVE ARTS

TUDOR AND STUART BRITAIN 1500-1714

Michael Snodin and John Styles

V&A Publications

First published by V&A Publications, 2004

V&A Publications
160 Brompton Road
London SW3 1HW

Originally published as part of
Design and the Decorative Arts: Britain 1500–1900, 2001

Designed by Janet James

ISBN 1 85177 420 3

A catalogue record for this book is available from the British Library.

Front cover illustration: Embroidered casket, 1671. Martha Edlin. VAM T.432–1990.
Back cover illustration: Design for armour and extra pieces, for Sir Henry Lee, 1570–5. Probably drawn by Jacob Halder. VAM D.599–1894.
Frontispiece: Chinese porcelain jar with English mounts; jar 1630–40, mounts 1660–70. VAM M.308–1962.
Contents page: The Heneage Jewel, about 1600. VAM M.81–1935.

Printed in Italy

V&A Publications
160 Brompton Road
London SW3 1HW
www.vam.ac.uk

Contents

Acknowledgements

Planning, writing and editing this book and its companion volumes was an integral part of the wider British Galleries project at the V&A. As the book's editors and principal authors, we owe a great debt of gratitude to Christopher Wilk, who led the British Galleries project, Alan Borg, former Director of the V&A, Gwyn Miles, Director of Projects & Estate, and to all the staff of the project, in particular to Nick Humphrey, in his role as the Tudor and Stuart Gallery Team Co-ordinator.

For ideas, references and advice on illustrations we are grateful to Cathy Arbuthnot, Justin Champion, Rosemany Crill, Richard Edgcumbe, Hazel Forsyth, Anthony Kersting, Roger Knight, Reino Liefkes, Sarah Medlam, Anthony North, Alex Werner, the late Clive Wainwright and James Yorke, as well as to all our fellow contributors. Thanks are also due to the many students on the V&A/RCA M.A. Course in the History of Design who have written relevant essays and dissertations, from which we learned much. We are grateful to Anthony Burton, Michael Braddick, Maurice Howard and Amanda Vickery for reading sections of the text and commenting on them.

We would like to thank the following people for their hard work and support: Mary Butler at V&A Publications and the team she assembled, especially project manager Geoff Barlow, copy-editor Mandy Greenfield, designer Janet James and indexer John Noble; the V&A's photographers and the staff of the V&A Picture Library; Kim Smith; Alicia Weisberg-Roberts; Paul Greenhalgh and Carolyn Sargentson.

Finally we must register our gratitude to our colleagues in the Department of Prints, Drawings and Paintings at the V&A and on the V&A/RCA M.A. Course in the History of Design, and most importantly, to our families. Thank you.

The book is dedicated to our fathers.

Michael Snodin and John Styles

Notes for Readers

For books and prints, the place of publication is London unless otherwise stated. For objects, the country of manufacture is Great Britain unless otherwise stated. Illustrations are numbered by chapter. Cross-references to illustrations take the form 3:12, the first number indicating the chapter, the second the illustration number. In the captions, h. indicates height, w. width, l. length and diam. diameter. Dimensions are provided only in those cases where the size of an object is unclear or is discussed in the text.

Foreword

This book originally appeared as the first section of *Design and the Decorative Arts: Britain 1500–1900*, the book published to complement and contextualize the Victoria and Albert Museum's new British Galleries 1500–1900, opened in November 2001. *Design and the Decorative Arts: Tudor and Stuart Britain 1500–1714* now appears as a separate paperback, alongside its Georgian and Victorian counterparts, to make the subject accessible to a wider audience.

Like the V&A's British Galleries, this book is primarily concerned with those apparently functional, but often deliberately aesthetically pleasing objects which fall between the traditional concerns of the fine arts and architecture. They include furniture, ceramics, metalwares, textiles and clothing, graphic works of various kinds, as well as the immensely varied products of manufacturing we associate with the phrase 'industrial design'. These are the objects which have come to constitute the territory of design in its most familiar modern usage.

The question of design is central to this book. The earliest meaning of the word in Britain was close to the Italian term *disegno* and was intimately linked to the activity of drawing. Thus a design was a drawing or print, and the activity of designing was to make a drawing which would enable a two- or three-dimensional object to be made, whether by hand, machine, or a combination of the two. More recently, the term design has often been used to refer exclusively to modern objects, especially those whose appearance was shaped by architects, industrial or product designers, by the tenets of twentieth-century Modernism, or the imperatives of industrial mass production. In this context the focus is on the final look of the object – its design. By contrast, historic objects like those in the V&A have been described as decorative, or applied, art. These are nineteenth-century terms which aimed to associate decorative, practical or utilitarian objects with the status of the fine arts, whilst continuing to differentiate them from it. The term decorative art, unlike applied art, still has popular currency and is therefore used in the title of this book.

Yet even before the nineteenth century, the word design could have the broader meaning of an intention, a plan, or a conception. Today it is this meaning which prevails when we use the word design in relation to objects. When we speak of an object's design we mean its overall characteristics and the processes that have taken place in order to create it. It is in this sense that the word design is employed in this book. The book identifies design as a complex and multi-layered process, including research, experimentation, manufacture, marketing and use, rather than concerning itself solely with the history of drawn or printed designs, or with the appearance of the finished object.

The V&A is Britain's National Museum of Art and Design. Its collections represent what people at various periods in the past – patrons, consumers, collectors, curators – have considered to be the best of their kind in aesthetic terms. This book, rooted as it is in the V&A's collections, reflects this history of institutional collecting. As a consequence, it deals principally with what are referred to as high-design objects. These were objects that embodied a deliberate striving after the most prized aesthetic effects of their era. They were made to be used by the economically and socially privileged whose tastes dictated what was considered beautiful and fashionable at any time. It was they who commanded the resources necessary to procure the most expensive materials and to enjoy the fruits of the most skilled techniques of manufacture. The book acknowledges that these high-design objects were only one element in the wider visual culture that prevailed in Tudor and Stuart Britain, a visual culture which in many of its more everyday aspects remains poorly understood. It is able to address a wider range of objects than the British Galleries and place them in a deeper historical context. Where possible, it makes reference to everyday objects and to the people for whom and by whom they were made.

The book is organized around four distinct but complementary questions: What were the formal aesthetics of different styles? Which people and institutions led taste? How did new modes of living lead to the design of new types of objects or the increased consumption of existing ones? What was new, in terms of products, materials and techniques of manufacture? Different questions might have been asked, but these four themes would inevitably form the core of them. It is not a book about the history of Tudor and Stuart Britain, although its introduction links design to that broader history. Nor is it a history of British designers, although many of them grace its pages. Rather it is a book about design in Tudor and Stuart Britain. It considers what was distinctively British about British design, but it also explores the import and creative adaptation of objects and visual ideas that originated elsewhere. Britain is taken to mean the territory of Great Britain, in other words England, Scotland and Wales.

CHAPTER 1

Introduction

JOHN STYLES

1. Stability and change

The rulers of Tudor and Stuart Britain prized order, hierarchy and stability, and yet the experience of the Tudor and Stuart period was one of profound change. The Protestant faith replaced the Catholic faith as the national religion; a civil war was fought and a king beheaded; the British Isles were brought together under a single ruler; plantations and trading posts were established in the Americas and Asia, across previously unsailed seas. Such changes, and the heightened sense of both impermanence and opportunity that they provoked, were not confined to the spheres of religion, politics and international relations. They extended to the material world inhabited by British men and women, to the works of art and the everyday things that shaped their lives. Britain's rulers tried intermittently to hold back the tide of material change, but in vain. Parliament enacted laws to confine the wearing of fashionable clothes to limited categories of people; monarchs issued royal proclamations to prevent the fields on the edges of London disappearing under new houses. Yet in the course of the sixteenth and seventeenth centuries the fashion cycle achieved an unprecedented intensity and London expanded to become the largest city in western Europe.

It is the mushrooming growth of London that offers the most vivid illustration of the material changes that transformed Tudor and Stuart Britain. London was the phenomenon of the age. In 1500, under the rule of the first Tudor king, Henry VII, it was a middle-ranking medieval capital city, inhabited by some 40,000 people. Its houses were built of timber, clay and plaster; its streets were narrow. In population, it was less than half the size of leading continental cities like Paris and Venice. In commerce, it was subservient to the vibrant mercantile centres of the Low Countries, particularly Bruges and Antwerp. In the course of the next hundred years London boomed, as trade, manufacturing and government all expanded. The sixteenth century

1 Detail of *Edward VI's processional entry into the City of London in 1547*. Painted in 1787 by Samuel Hieronymous Grimm after a wall painting at Cowdray House, Sussex, now lost. Watercolour. Society of Antiquaries of London.

witnessed what the 1615 edition of John Stow's *Annales, or, a General Chronicle of England* described as 'the unimaginable enlarging of London, and the suburbs, within the space of fiftie years'. By the time the last Tudor monarch, Elizabeth I, died in 1603, the city had more than quadrupled in size, housing approximately 180,000 people.

But in its physical appearance Shakespeare's London was still a medieval city, not a Renaissance one. It resembled its smaller, early-Tudor predecessor of a century before more than it did contemporary continental cities like Antwerp, Venice or even Paris. Despite spectacular growth in the city's population, buildings in new architectural styles, like the Royal Exchange in Cornhill, closely modelled on the bourse in Antwerp, or the classical façade of Somerset House on the Strand, were the exception, not the rule. In the case of the Royal Exchange, it was not simply the design but also the designer, Hendrick van Paesschen, and much of the building material that came from Flanders. Few London houses were built of brick, and the formal entrances to the city – its gates – were old-fashioned and lacked magnificence, while its parish churches were outdated and in poor repair. In 1561 the spire of St Paul's Cathedral had been struck by lightning and burned; by 1603 it had still not

2 Detail of *Londinium*, a design for a triumphal arch made for the procession of James I and VI through the City of London in March 1604. Engraved by William Kip and published by Stephen Harrison as part of the set, *Arch's of Triumph*, 1604. The scene depicted is London at the start of the 17th century. Engraving. VAM 14006.

3 *Byrsa Londinensis vulgo the Royal Exchange,* 1647. Engraved by Wenceslaus Hollar. Building designed by Hendrick van Paesschen. The engraving shows the Exchange as built in 1566–71, before its destruction in the Great Fire of 1666. Engraving. VAM E.2203-1948.

been replaced. The city lacked fine vistas and public spaces like those that had recently been created in Antwerp, Rome and Paris.

When Queen Anne, the last Stuart monarch, died in 1714, all this had changed. London had overtaken Paris as the largest city in western Europe, with a population of nearly 600,000. It was about to displace Amsterdam as the centre of the world's trading economy. Moreover, London had been physically transformed. A guide book published in 1708 could describe the city as 'the most spatious, populous, rich, beautiful, renowned and noble that we know of at this day in the world'. The journalist and author Daniel Defoe, writing shortly after Queen Anne's death, observed 'new squares and new streets rising up every day to such a prodigy of buildings that nothing in the world does, or ever did, equal it, except old Rome in Trajan's time'.

In part, this physical transformation was a consequence of the Great Fire of London, which razed vast tracts of the city in 1666. The speed with which the burned-out areas were rebuilt is testimony to London's astonishing wealth in the second half of the seventeenth century. The quality of the public buildings that replaced those destroyed in the Fire, most prominently the 52 new churches, demonstrates the mastery of the classical style achieved by native British architects, in particular Christopher Wren. But the ravages of the Fire accounted for only some of the new building that changed the face of London in the half-century after 1660. The distinctive new residential squares extolled by Defoe – Panton Square, Soho Square, St James's Square, Red Lion Square, Leicester Square, Bloomsbury Square – were developed principally in the West End of the metropolis, which the Fire never reached.

This new London, this new world city, was not a planned exercise in baroque pomp and magnificence, the brainchild of an absolute monarch. It lacked the monuments and palaces, the vistas of cathedrals and citadels that were to typify the aesthetics of royal absolutism in Turin, Karlsruhe and Berlin. Moreover, there was no British Versailles, no purpose-built royal seat of government located at a safe but accessible distance from the capital. In these and many other of its physical characteristics, Queen Anne's London was a reflection of the chequered history of the nation and its capital under the

4 *Sohoe or King's Square,* 1754. Drawn by Edward Days, engraved by Sutton Nicholls. Originally known as King's Square, Soho Square was developed in the 1680s. Engraving. VAM E.624-1976.

Tudors and Stuarts. That history was one of sustained economic expansion, combined with political inconsistency and often discord, which foreigners found baffling. The city's out-of-date and half-completed royal palaces were testimony to the way in which the power and wealth of successive monarchs had waxed and waned. It was Wren's new churches that dominated the city's skyline, proclaiming the hard-won but still qualified ascendancy of that peculiarly British brand of Protestantism embodied in the Church of England. The mercantile heart of the city, quickly reconstructed after the Fire in a piecemeal fashion, ignoring the grand formal replanning advocated by Wren and others, attested to the overwhelming priority that London's merchant rulers accorded to the continuation of business as usual. The elegant new streets and squares of the West End were evidence of the commercial disposition of the British nobility, eager to turn a profit from its landed property on the fringes of the city by providing wealthy people from across the British Isles with the smart London residences they craved.

6

5

5 *The Thames at Horseferry*, about 1706–10. By Jan Griffier the Elder. In the background is the City of London, where the spires of Wren's churches flank the newly completed dome of St Paul's Cathedral. Oil on canvas. The Museum of London.

6 *The Palace of Whitehall*, after a mid-17th-century engraving by Wenceslaus Hollar. Published by William Herbert, 1809. The Banqueting House on the left was built in 1619–22 to a design by Inigo Jones. Subsequently, Charles I planned a new royal palace around it in the same classical style, but it was never built. The Banqueting House was still surrounded by much older buildings when Charles I was beheaded in 1649 on a scaffold erected in front of it. Engraving. VAM E.416-1898.

2. The medieval legacy

In 1500, at the end of what we now call the Middle Ages, Britain played a peripheral role in the affairs of Europe. What contemporaries saw as the great centres of European art and culture, of wealth and power, lay elsewhere. It was the beautiful objects created in places like Venice and Florence, Antwerp and Bruges that were coveted throughout western Europe, not those made in London. Foreigners saw little that was admirable – or even worthy of comment – in English decorative art and design. What we now perceive as the triumphs of the visual arts in fifteenth-century England, particularly the Perpendicular style in architecture, were uniquely English and had negligible influence elsewhere in Europe. What was true of England was even more true of Scotland and Wales, which had far smaller populations.

If England held a peripheral place in European cultural affairs at the end of the Middle Ages, this state of affairs reflected its marginality in economic and political matters. The centres of gravity of European trade and urban life lay in the Low Countries and the Mediterranean. Indeed, the British Isles lay towards the geographical margins of the world as it was then understood by Europeans. The Atlantic Ocean was perceived as the boundary of the known world, not as a gateway to global intercourse. It was only in 1492 that Christopher Columbus, financed by the King and Queen of Spain, landed in the Americas; it was only in 1498 that the Portuguese Vasco da Gama reached India by sea. In 1500, moreover, England's direct stake in continental European affairs was much reduced. The vast swathes of French territory that the kings of England had controlled during most of the later Middle Ages were entirely lost in the course of the fifteenth

century. By 1500 England had been stripped of all its possessions in continental Europe, with the single exception of Calais. In 1529, Henry VIII, not known for his modesty, described himself as 'a small king in a corner' of Europe. At home, the political turmoil of the Wars of the Roses between 1455 and 1487 limited the capacity of court and nobility to exercise cultural leadership. England enjoyed fertile soils and mineral wealth, but it was thinly populated. Its population in 1500, at under two and a half million, had hardly recovered from the losses inflicted by the 'Black Death' of more than a century before. Foreigners commented on the country's natural wealth, but criticized its people's reluctance to exert themselves to enhance it.

7 King's College chapel, Cambridge, built 1446–1515. The Perpendicular style of architecture at its grandest.

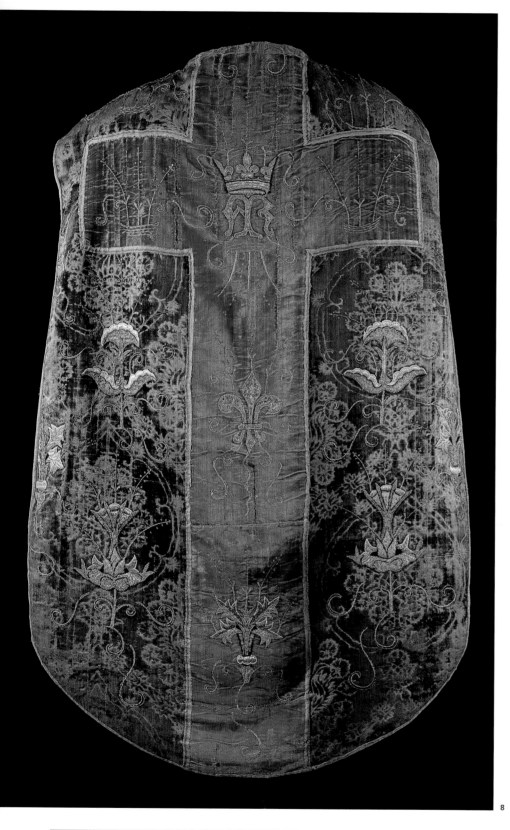

In both manufactures and trade England was underdeveloped compared with the leading European centres. Her economy was overwhelmingly agricultural and her towns were small. She was Europe's main supplier of woollen cloth, but the cloth was exported in an undyed, semi-finished state, and trade in this staple commodity was becoming entirely controlled from Antwerp. Woollen cloth was the country's only major export. The highest-quality luxury goods were largely imported. In 1436 the English were already complaining about 'the great galees of Venees and Florence' that brought 'thynges wyth whiche they fetely blere oure eye, wyth thynges not endurynge that we bye'. This flow of foreign luxuries testifies to the country's wealth and the desire of the wealthy to spend on fine goods. But to secure them the wealthy, including the King, had to rely on the skills of immigrants from continental Europe. Native English producers of such goods were largely incapable of performing to the highest western European standards of technique and aesthetic quality. The range of goods that they could make was narrow and the techniques they employed were limited. Innovation came predominantly from abroad.

9

8

8 Chasuble, 1480–1538. A pre-Reformation priest's vestment made partly of imported Italian silk. Silk velvet; embroidery on linen applied to the velvet, with silver-gilt and silk threads with sequins. The silk velvet probably made in Italy, embroidered in England. VAM Loan: Butler-Bowden.3.

9 *Henry VII*, about 1509–11. Sculpted in London by the Florentine sculptor Pietro Torrigiani. Painted terracotta. VAM A.49-1935.

10 The Heneage ('Armada') Jewel, about 1600. The medallic image portrays Elizabeth I. Gold and enamel, with diamonds and rubies. VAM M.81-1935.

10

3. Authority

In the course of the sixteenth and seventeenth centuries, the marginal position occupied by Britain in European cultural affairs at the end of the Middle Ages was reversed. By the early eighteenth century British makers of a range of high-design goods could perform to the highest European standards. London had become one of the continent's leading centres for design and the decorative arts. This cultural transformation did not take place in isolation. It went hand-in-hand with the rise of British political and economic influence in Europe and beyond. But Britain's acquisition of political and economic power was hard-won. Political life in Tudor and Stuart Britain was turbulent, unpredictable and could be bloody. Foreigners found British politics confusing, inconsistent and sometimes incomprehensible. 'Since the time of Queen Elizabeth,' Johan de Witt, the leading Dutch politician of his age, was quoted as saying in 1668, there had been 'only a continual fluctuation in the conduct of England, with which one could not concert measures for two years at a time'. Nevertheless, it is possible to identify three fundamental political issues that had particular significance for developments in design and the decorative arts under the Tudors and Stuarts. The first was the problem of

11

constitutional authority, the second the problem of religion, and the third the problem of international relations. Each was intimately linked to the others.

For most of the sixteenth and seventeenth centuries Britain was subject to a system of government in which the monarch was pivotal. Indeed, under the Tudors the powers of the English Crown increased. The experience of turmoil during the Wars of the Roses had rendered a strong monarchy attractive to many of the great landowners as a guarantee of order and privilege. In the sixteenth century persistent threats from abroad – from Scotland, France, the Pope and Spain – added to the appeal of strong leadership. The Protestant Reformation under Henry VIII made the monarch the spiritual as well as the secular head of the realm. Order and obedience became an obsession among the governing classes; the sovereign power of the monarch was exalted as the fount of all authority. By the end of the sixteenth century writers could describe the Queen, Elizabeth I, as an absolute monarch. Her successor, James I and VI, claimed to rule by divine right.

The power of the monarchy under the Tudors and Stuarts was not unlimited, however, either in theory or in practice. Even in theory, it had long been the prevailing view that England's was a mixed constitution, under which the King was expected to rule in cooperation with his subjects as represented in Parliament. That Parliament was far from being a democratically elected body, but in a rough and ready manner it did represent the wealthier and more powerful sections of the population across the realm. By continental European standards, the powers of the English Parliament were already considerable at the start of the sixteenth century. Parliament's authority grew under the Tudors, in particular because Henry VIII relied on it to force through the Protestant Reformation. By the seventeenth century, when continental monarchs increasingly chose to disregard whatever institutions existed to represent their subjects, the authority exercised by the English Parliament had become exceptional, even if it was not unique.

11 *James I and VI and his family*, 1612–14. Painted in the studios of Nicholas Hilliard and Isaac Oliver and assembled about 1625–50. These portraits were painted separately, but framed together soon afterwards. From top left: *James*; *Anne of Denmark*, his queen; *Prince Henry*, his son and heir who died in 1612; *Prince Charles*; *Frederick King of Bohemia*, his son-in-law; and *Elizabeth*, *Queen of Bohemia*, his daughter. Watercolour on vellum, in a 17th-century frame of ebony veneered onto oak. VAM P.147-152-1910.

TUDOR AND STUART MONARCHS, 1485–1714

John Styles

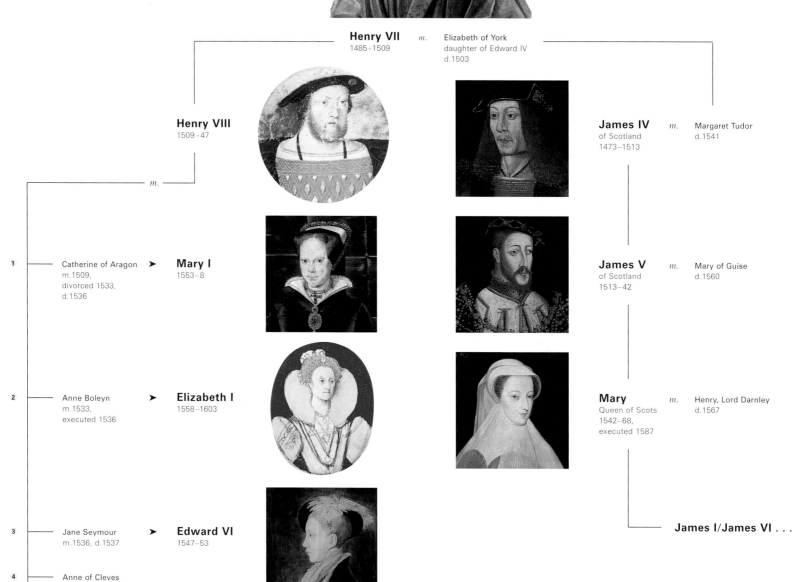

Henry VII   *m.*   Elizabeth of York
1485–1509   daughter of Edward IV
                           d.1503

Henry VIII
1509–47

James IV   *m.*   Margaret Tudor
of Scotland   d.1541
1473–1513

m.

1   Catherine of Aragon   ➤   **Mary I**
    m.1509,   1553–8
    divorced 1533,
    d.1536

James V   *m.*   Mary of Guise
of Scotland   d.1560
1513–42

2   Anne Boleyn   ➤   **Elizabeth I**
    m.1533,   1558–1603
    executed 1536

Mary   *m.*   Henry, Lord Darnley
Queen of Scots   d.1567
1542–68,
executed 1587

3   Jane Seymour   ➤   **Edward VI**
    m.1536, d.1537   1547–53

                                          James I/James VI . . .

4   Anne of Cleves
    m.1540, divorced 1541, d.1557

5   Katherine Howard
    m.1541, executed 1542

6   Catherine Parr
    m.1543, d.1548

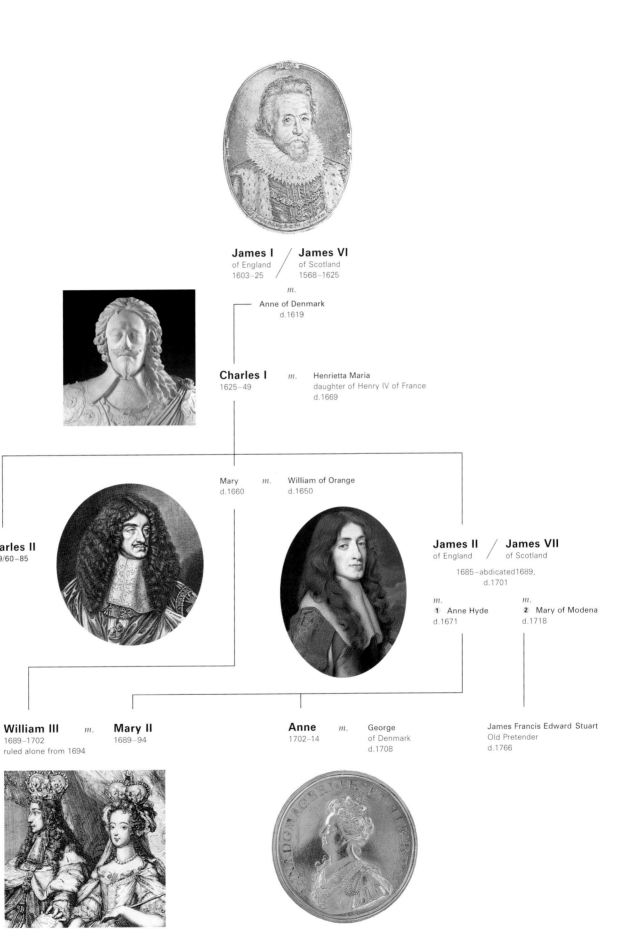

James I / **James VI**
of England / of Scotland
1603–25 / 1568–1625

m.

Anne of Denmark
d.1619

Charles I   *m.*   Henrietta Maria
1625–49   daughter of Henry IV of France
                           d.1669

Mary   *m.*   William of Orange
d.1660   d.1650

Catherine of Braganza   *m.*   **Charles II**
d.1705   1649/60–85

James II / **James VII**
of England / of Scotland

1685–abdicated1689,
d.1701

m.   *m.*
1 Anne Hyde   **2** Mary of Modena
d.1671   d.1718

William III   *m.*   **Mary II**
1689–1702   1689–94
ruled alone from 1694

Anne   *m.*   George
1702–14   of Denmark
                     d.1708

James Francis Edward Stuart
Old Pretender
d.1766

Parliament, moreover, was not the only constraint on the power of the Crown. In contrast to continental monarchs like Philip II of Spain and Louis XIII of France, the Tudors and their immediate Stuart successors in England had no professional army and no professional civil service to impose their will. For most of the period these were luxuries they could not afford. Henry VIII had inherited vast landed estates. He supplemented their income with that of the lands he confiscated from the monasteries dissolved in 1536 and 1539. But this carefully assembled royal wealth was rapidly dissipated in that most expensive of royal pursuits – warfare. Henry's own wars with France, his daughter Elizabeth's war with Spain and her campaigns in Ireland left the royal coffers almost bare. Parliament could, and did, grant additional revenue from taxation for war and other emergencies, but it did so only reluctantly and with conditions attached, which monarchs often found irksome. Nevertheless, expectations of government continued to grow, as did the cost of warfare as firearms replaced longbows and pikes. By the early seventeenth century the Stuart kings could make ends meet only if they avoided expensive wars and extravagant expenditure at court. For much of the 1630s Charles I's income was as little as one-tenth of Louis XIII's.

Charles I's ineptitude in managing these problems of royal authority and finance helped bring about the civil war of the 1640s, but neither the war nor Charles's beheading in 1649, nor even Oliver Cromwell's republican regime in the 1650s, successfully resolved them. For all the enthusiastic royalism displayed by Parliament in the aftermath of the restoration of Charles II in 1660, similar problems quickly re-emerged. They were finally resolved only after the overthrow of Charles II's brother, James II and VII, in what its victorious supporters called the 'Glorious Revolution' of 1688. James was toppled from the throne in that year by an invasion of Dutch troops led by his son-in-law, William of Orange, military leader of the Netherlands. William's

His Excellencie, Oliuer Cromwell, Generall of all the Forces of England, Scotland, & Ireland, Chancelour of the Vniverſity of Oxford, Lord Protector of England, Scotland and Ireland.

R.G. fecit.   Peter Stent Exc: 1653.

13

12 Wheel-lock pistol and powder-flask, about 1580. Made in England. Steel, wooden stock inlaid with engraved staghorn, and barrel mounts damascened in gold and silver. VAM M.949-1983 and M.950-1983.

13 *Oliver Cromwell*, 1653. After a drawing by Robert Gaywood. Etching. VAM E.1348-1960.

priority was to secure British support in his war with Louis XIV's France. In return for that support, he was prepared to accept a dramatic and, as it turned out, decisive tilting of the balance of constitutional authority in Britain away from the monarch towards Parliament. Henceforth British monarchs ruled on terms dictated by the legislature. Parliament had become the ultimate source of political authority. Claims to absolute monarchy and the divine right of kings could no longer be sustained. The ceremonial life of the royal court continued, but it was no longer to be the focus of authority, either political or cultural.

14 James II and VII crowned by Peace and Justice, about 1685. By Jacobus Constantin. Ivory; frame of tortoiseshell and ebony. VAM A.13-1937.

15 Terracotta model of William III, about 1695. By Jan van Nost the Elder. This figure is a model for a full-size statue of the King that was erected in 1695 at the Royal Exchange in London. Modelled terracotta. VAM A.35-1939.

For much of the Tudor and Stuart period, therefore, there was a mismatch between the authority that British monarchs believed they should exercise and their capacity to do so. This was as true of the artistic realm as it was in matters of domestic governance or foreign policy. In art, as in war, expectations were set not in Britain, but in continental Europe. Rulers in Italy, Germany, Spain and France, many of them uninhibited by the constitutional limitations that applied in England, established new and ever more costly standards of royal splendour. Renaissance and baroque kingship was extraordinarily theatrical. Monarchs and their courtiers lavished their subjects' wealth on palaces and paintings, furnishings and festivals designed to outshine their rivals, both at home and abroad. Displays of material magnificence and aloof grandeur were deliberately contrived to inspire awe, to project authority and to foster obedience. The impresarios of this orgy of courtly display were artists and craftspeople, architects and designers; its settings were royal palaces and royal progresses.

However much Britain's Tudor and Stuart monarchs aspired to match the leading European kings and emperors in splendour and magnificence, few of them succeeded. The monarch who came closest was Henry VIII, who regarded himself as the equal of major European rulers like Francis I of France and enjoyed, at some points in his reign at least, financial resources sufficient to compete aesthetically as well as diplomatically and militarily. His expensive new palaces were lavishly decorated by foreign artists, adopting elements of new styles derived from continental Europe. But in the first half of the sixteenth century the royal court numbered only about 1,000 people and the costs of international competition in architectural and artistic magnificence were still limited. None of Henry's Tudor or Stuart successors was as successful in matching the aesthetic grandeur achieved by their foremost continental rivals. Whether through lack of money, lack of will or lack of time, none of them managed to complete the building of an entirely new royal palace. Yet the physical need for such a palace became all the more pressing as the size of the court, 'greater and more gallant' than before, grew to nearly 2,000 people by the 1630s.

Of all Henry VIII's successors, it was the ill-fated Charles I who came closest to the Renaissance ideal of kingship in his aesthetic policy. Profoundly conscious of the capacity of art, architecture and design to project the dignity and majesty of monarchy, Charles built, commissioned and collected. He was himself a connoisseur and, like many of his courtiers, displayed a knowledge of continental art and design that was unprecedented in its sophistication. In 1629 the Flemish artist Peter Paul Rubens was struck by the 'incredible quality of excellent pictures, statues and ancient inscriptions

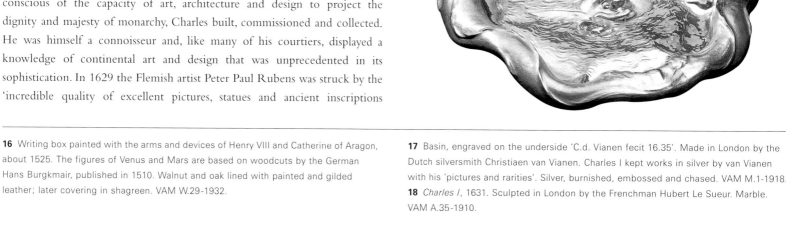

16 Writing box painted with the arms and devices of Henry VIII and Catherine of Aragon, about 1525. The figures of Venus and Mars are based on woodcuts by the German Hans Burgkmair, published in 1510. Walnut and oak lined with painted and gilded leather; later covering in shagreen. VAM W.29-1932.

17 Basin, engraved on the underside 'C.d. Vianen fecit 16.35'. Made in London by the Dutch silversmith Christiaen van Vianen. Charles I kept works in silver by van Vianen with his 'pictures and rarities'. Silver, burnished, embossed and chased. VAM M.1-1918.
18 *Charles I*, 1631. Sculpted in London by the Frenchman Hubert Le Sueur. Marble. VAM A.35-1910.

which are to be found in this court'. He found 'none of the crudeness which one might expect from a place so remote from Italian elegance'. Charles's principal designer, Inigo Jones, and other leading courtiers had been to Italy and studied Italian design. The King spent on architecture and high design even when his resources were pinched, laying out £133,000 to complete the Queen's House at Greenwich at a time in the 1630s when his debts were rising. But the money and effort that Charles invested in the aesthetics of royal power entirely failed to prevent his own downfall and, at least temporarily, that of the monarchy. Under the Cromwellian republic, royal palaces were sold off, as was most of Charles's prized collection of paintings.

19 The south front of the Queen's House, Greenwich, London, built 1616–35. Designed by Inigo Jones.

20 Cabinet, 1644–50. Made in Florence for John Evelyn with panels by Domenico Benotti and bronze plaques by Francesco Fanelli. Evelyn, an active royalist, travelled extensively in France and Italy between 1643 and 1652. In Florence he bought hard-stone floral panels and had them incorporated into this cabinet, possibly adding the bronze plaques later. Collecting was a new, fashionable activity at Charles I's court, and cabinets were display cases for art treasures and curiosities. Ebony veneer on a pine carcase with panels of pietra dura, oak drawers, gilt-bronze mounts and plaques; later brass strawberry-leaf cresting. VAM W. 24-1977.

BRITAIN AND ITS RULERS, 1485–1714

John Styles

In 1485 Henry Tudor defeated and killed Richard III at the Battle of Bosworth to become King Henry VII of England (1485–1509) and establish the Tudor dynasty on the English throne. At this date the different political entities that made up the British Isles – England, Ireland, Scotland and Wales – were politically quite distinct. England and Scotland were entirely separate kingdoms, with different royal families (the Tudors in England and the Stewarts in Scotland), although there was a long-standing claim of overlordship in Scotland by the Kings of England. Wales comprised a principality and a march under English control. The Kings of England claimed the Lordship of Ireland, but in practice their authority was limited to areas in the east and south of that country.

Two hundred and thirty years later, on the death of Queen Anne (1702–14), the last Stuart monarch, the political organization of the British Isles had been transformed. A single monarch ruled all the territories in the British archipelago and the work of governing those territories was subject to effective central oversight from London, although distinct political institutions still operated in Scotland and Ireland.

The process of integration was begun by the second Tudor King of England, Henry VIII (1509–47). Laws were made in England in 1536 and 1543 to unite England and Wales as a single kingdom. Wales was divided into counties and granted representation in the English Parliament. This was not an act of union ratified by both parties, but rather an imposition by the English of their law and customs. Wales became part of England as far as its political institutions were concerned, although the Tudors (who had Welsh roots) did go on to promote the idea of Britain, with its links to Arthurian legend and the pre-Saxon era. In addition, in 1541 Henry VIII had Ireland

designated a kingdom and himself proclaimed its king. The kingdom of Ireland remained, however, an entity separate from England, with its own council, parliament and courts in Dublin. It was to remain so until the nineteenth century.

When Elizabeth I (1558–1603), the last Tudor monarch of England and Ireland, died without children, her successor was James VI of Scotland (1568–1625). He became James I of England and Ireland and anglicized the spelling of his family name to Stuart. The uniting of the Scottish and English crowns was accompanied by the use of the term 'Great Britain' to describe the new joint entity. James was anxious to move rapidly towards a full political union of the two kingdoms, to be symbolized by the creation of a new union flag combining the crosses of St George for England and St Andrew for Scotland. Various designs were proposed, but it was one that superimposed the cross of St George on the cross of St Andrew that was eventually adopted in 1606. It still forms the basis of the modern Union Jack.

Choosing a design for the new flag proved easier than creating an effective political union between the two nations. The English Parliament refused to support James's desire for steps towards a full political union of the kingdoms of England and Scotland and there the matter rested for half a century. A political union of the two countries was imposed briefly between 1654 and 1660 by the republican government of Oliver Cromwell, which came to power in the aftermath of the English civil war (1642–6) and the execution of James I's son, Charles I (1625–49). With the Restoration of the monarchy in 1660, the two kingdoms became, once again, separate entities sharing only a monarch. The final union of Scotland and England to form the kingdom of Great Britain was agreed by the parliaments of the two countries in 1707.

21. Designs for an Anglo-Scottish union flag commissioned by Lord Admiral Nottingham, about 1604. Nottingham preferred the one that showed the crosses of St George and St Andrew side by side, 'for this is like man and wife, without blemish on to other', although none of them was adopted. Pen, ink and wash. National Library of Scotland.

22

23

4. Religion

The civil war that led to Charles I's execution was not, of course, simply the outcome of long-standing constitutional tensions between Crown and Parliament. It was also the product of disagreements about religion, which were equally deep-seated. The sixteenth century saw the adoption of the reformed, Protestant form of Christianity in England, Wales and Scotland. Reformation involved a rejection of the authority of the Pope in Rome, but it did not inaugurate freedom of conscience in religious affairs. One state-enforced religious monopoly was replaced by another. The beliefs and practices of the medieval Catholic Church centred on priestly rituals employing objects and images. Protestantism substituted forms of religious observance that centred on the word of God.

At the heart of sixteenth-century Protestantism was the Bible, printed in the vernacular using the technology of movable type, itself relatively new to Britain. Reformation, especially for its most enthusiastic devotees, required the destruction of the apparatus of Catholic ritual – the smashing and confiscation of the candlesticks, statues, altars, crucifixes, vestments and chalices in which popular belief and artistic skill had been invested in the Middle Ages. Iconoclasm fostered by the new Bible-based religion was more limited in England than it was in Scotland. In England the churches were not entirely stripped of ritual objects. Indeed, many English churches at the end of the sixteenth century retained elements of the look of their Catholic predecessors. Nevertheless, the Reformation fundamentally changed the nature of the rituals in which religious objects were employed, and worked to undermine belief in their spiritual potency. By doing so, it contributed to a secularization of design and the decorative arts. Never again would church patronage and the production of religious objects loom so large in the work of both artists and designers.

Protestantism had originated in the protests against the Roman Church started in 1517 in Germany by Martin Luther. In England and Scotland the new faith was imposed on the mass of the population without their consent, but it arrived in the two countries by different means and took different forms. In Scotland, Protestantism spread among sections of the population from the 1530s, but the decisive moment came in 1560 when Protestant nobles seized control of government in an anti-Catholic revolt that led to the expulsion of the Catholic Mary, Queen of Scots. During the long minority of her young son, James VI, the ruling nobles imposed a militant Presbyterian Protestantism as the state religion. The new Scottish church was organized around congregations. It was suspicious of interference from worldly authority, whether royal or ecclesiastical, and extremely hostile to religious images and icons. In England, by contrast, the reformed church was the creation of a king – Henry VIII – who had at first been hostile to Luther. Henry's break with Rome in 1533 was driven principally by his desire to divorce his first wife,

---

22 *St Agatha and St William of Norwich*. Part of a rood screen painted 1450–70 for the Chapel of St Mary in St John's Church, Maddermarket, Norwich. In a pre-Reformation church the whole congregation looked towards the rood screen, which separated priest and altar from the people. Tempera on oak panel. VAM 24-1894.

23 Communion cup and cover, with the royal arms, with London hallmarks for 1549–50. Maker's mark of W. An early example of post-Reformation church plate, from the period when plain Protestant communion cups began to replace the ornate chalices used in the Catholic mass. Silver-gilt and champlevé enamel. VAM Loan Aldermary 18a.

24 Title page to *The Bible in Englyshe*, 1540. Henry VIII is depicted as supreme head of the Church of England, enthroned beneath a tiny God the Father. He distributes copies of the Bible to the Archbishop of Canterbury and his chief minister, Thomas Cromwell, who pass them on to the bishops and lords. The crowds at the bottom of the page acclaim the King. Woodcut. The British Library.

25 Defaced painting of the Annunciation, 1470–90. From the Church of the Holy Innocents, Great Barton, Suffolk. Adapted from a traditional composition of the Virgin Mary enthroned, to represent the Annunciation by the addition of the words 'Ecce ancilla domini'. The careful erasing of the face may represent a post-Reformation effort to rob the traditional image of its power, while leaving it in its original position in the church. Tempera or oil on panel. VAM W.50-1921.

Catherine of Aragon. He became supreme governor of a church that retained a full ecclesiastical hierarchy with most of its powers. The King's commitment to Protestant ideas remained half-hearted. For the rest of the sixteenth century the reformed English church continued to display many features that disappointed Protestant militants.

It was governments that set the process of Reformation in motion, but, on both sides of the Anglo-Scottish border, inculcating Protestant belief among the population at large took time. Despite sustained persecution, pockets of Catholic resistance persisted, especially where local lords and gentry remained loyal to the old faith. Nevertheless, by the early seventeenth century large sections of the population of both countries were coming to consider themselves Protestants. In the face of bitter hostility from the Catholic powers of Europe – especially Spain – English popular nationalism began to take on that aggressively Protestant aspect that was to persist into the twentieth century. Foreigners came to regard the people of Britain as stridently Protestant. Protestant refugees, including many skilled craftspeople, flocked to Britain to escape persecution by Catholic rulers on the continent.

But the Reformation's legacy in terms of organization and doctrine was an inconsistent one. The militantly Presbyterian state church in Scotland existed alongside a hierarchical English church in which Protestant beliefs of various degrees coexisted, sometimes uneasily. In a world where it was commonly believed that good government required the enforcement of religious truth, these inconsistencies were disturbing. The union of the crowns of England and Scotland in 1603 highlighted them. The accession of Charles I, a king of deeply autocratic instincts, rendered them unsustainable. Charles sought to impose on both the English and Scottish churches a form of high-church Protestantism that extolled hierarchy, ritual and the divine right of monarchs. It involved a renewed emphasis on the trappings of worship, as opposed to preaching the word of God. This version of Protestantism, though still distinct from the Roman faith, did not seem very different from Catholicism to Scottish Presbyterians and their ultra-Protestant

26

sympathizers in England, the Puritans. Their concern was heightened by the success in turning back the tide of Protestantism enjoyed by a re-invigorated, Counter-Reformation Catholicism on the continent. British Protestants' suspicion of a Catholic conspiracy at Charles I's court was reinforced by Charles's marriage to Henrietta Maria, a French Catholic princess, for reasons of international dynastic politics. Hostility and paranoia provoked by Charles's religious policy, especially in Scotland, helped precipitate the civil war.

The religious policies of the Puritan victors in the civil war were no more successful than those of their royal predecessors, and they lost many supporters both by tolerating Protestant extremists and by attempting to reform morals and manners. With the restoration of Charles II in 1660, his father's brand of high-church Protestantism was re-established as the doctrine of the Church of England, to wide acclaim. It was soon to find impressive physical expression in Wren's new London churches. The Puritans and others, like the Quakers, who could not stomach the new religious order withdrew from the Church of England to establish their own dissenting congregations, which faced intermittent persecution. They comprised perhaps one-tenth of the population. Yet at the same time the two men who were the supreme rulers of the Church of England between 1660 and 1688, Charles II and James II and VII,

27

26 Communion cup and cover, with date letter for 1640. Maker's mark of RB. Acquired by Sir Robert Shirley for his family chapel at Staunton Harold, Leicestershire. The Gothic Revival style and the cross indicate Shirley's high-church Anglicanism, as does the engraving on the cup: 'MY BLOOD IS DRINKE INDEED'. During the civil war he remained a staunch royalist. Silver-gilt, engraved. VAM Loan: NT Staunton 5:1.

27 'The Plot first hatcht at Rome by the Pope and Cardinalls &ct.', one of a set of tiles depicting the Popish Plot, about 1679–80. The fictitious Popish Plot of 1678 involved an international Jesuit conspiracy to assassinate Charles II and place his overtly Catholic brother James on the throne. The widespread panic it occasioned is testimony to the extent of public paranoia about Catholicism in high places. Tin-glazed earthenware. VAM 414:823/1-1885.

either sympathized with the outlawed Catholic faith or, in the case of James, professed it. The sons of a Catholic mother, Charles and James had spent time in exile in Catholic Europe in the aftermath of the English civil war. They were admirers of the absolutist style of baroque Catholic monarchy practised by their cousin Louis XIV in France. James's authoritarian attempt to re-establish Catholicism in the mainstream of British life led directly to his forced abdication and return to exile in the 'Glorious Revolution' of 1688.

In its aftermath the assumption that all the King's subjects must profess the same faith was abandoned. Under William and Mary, freedom of worship was extended to all Protestants. Britain became in effect a multi-denominational society. This did not mean religious equality. A state church continued to exist, enjoying enormous political, economic and organizational privileges. Other Protestant denominations had to finance their own clergy and premises. In England, the state church was Anglican; in Scotland it was Presbyterian – a cynical but realistic accommodation to national differences in theology that marked a retreat from the commitment to religious uniformity of previous generations. Henceforth even the tiny minority of Catholics, who remained subject to legal proscription, were by and large left in peace.

28 *Charles II giving audience to the Governors, masters and children of Christ's Hospital*, about 1680. By Antonio Verrio. Preliminary sketch for the 'Great Picture' at Christ's Hospital, a charity school. Oil on canvas. VAM P.2-1956.

5. Britain in the wider world

Western Europe in the sixteenth and seventeenth centuries was a dangerous place. Divided then, much more than it is now, into a multiplicity of different states, the continent was beset with rivalries and conflicts that intermingled domestic and foreign affairs in a peculiarly intimate way. Religious hostility between Protestant and Catholic was rife both within states and between them, as the Reformation swept northern Europe and the Counter-Reformation then strove to extirpate it. Absolute monarchs were pitted against representative institutions at home and abroad. In a Europe where most states were monarchies and the various royal families, disdainful of inferiors, intermarried endlessly, the claims and counter-claims of competing royal dynasties were a constant theme of domestic and international politics. Economic rivalries, driven by the spiralling costs of warfare and inspired by dreams of unimaginable riches in the newly explored world beyond Europe, led to a merging of trade, war and overseas expansion on a global scale.

The disputes over constitutional authority and religion that bedevilled Tudor and Stuart Britain were all the more potent, therefore, because they involved choices that had international as well as domestic ramifications. Choosing Protestantism came to mean antagonizing Catholic Spain, the most powerful state in western Europe in the sixteenth century, fuelled by wealth from its American conquests. Upholding a mixed, parliamentary constitution meant rejecting the alternative – the authoritarian, absolutist form of kingship, which seemed to many Europeans the most modern and effective form of government, especially as practised by Louis XIV of France in the later seventeenth century. The expansion of trade and colonies involved conflict not only with Catholic, absolutist Spain, which claimed a monopoly in the Americas, but also with the Protestant, anti-absolutist Dutch, who became the

dominant commercial power in the seventeenth century. The outcomes of these difficult and often contradictory choices were not simply religious, political and economic. For most of this period Britain played a peripheral role in the setting of international trends in design and the decorative arts. It was a taker rather than a setter of fashion and taste. Religious, economic or political choices could influence which foreign aesthetic influences prevailed in Britain – French rather than Spanish styles in dress, Protestant rather than Catholic refugee craftspeople.

Despite all the confusing twists and turns of British policy, the long-term trajectory of Britain's international position is clear enough. At the start of the sixteenth century England was a small-to-middling European power. Its only overseas territory, Calais, was lost in 1557. Britain as a whole played only a minor part in the spectacular sixteenth-century projection of European power into Africa, Asia and the Americas, which was undertaken principally by Portugal and Spain. Two centuries later Great Britain was, along with France, one of the two leading contenders for world power. Underpinned by the growth of agriculture, trade and manufactures evident from the mid-sixteenth century onwards, British military capacity began to make an impact on the world stage under Oliver Cromwell in the 1650s. After the Glorious Revolution, the new constitutional settlement enabled Britain's economic resources to be translated into military might much more effectively. By 1714, after some twenty years of warfare, the armies of the British and their allies, led by the Duke of Marlborough, had defeated Louis XIV's expansionist, aggressively Catholic France, the largest and most powerful state in continental Europe. In the course of the seventeenth century Britain had also acquired an extra-European empire – Barbados and Jamaica in the West Indies; a string of colonies along the eastern seaboard of North America, from Newfoundland in the north to the Carolinas in the south; Bombay and Madras in India; and, early in the eighteenth century, a semi-permanent trading presence at Canton in China.

Britain's international standing in design and the decorative arts followed a parallel trajectory. At the start of the sixteenth century they exhibited a provincialism characterized by an overwhelming dependence on ideas, people and objects from the Low Countries. In the course of the sixteenth and especially the seventeenth centuries provincialism gradually came to be replaced by a cosmopolitan confidence, which saw Britain acquire, rework and increasingly re-market aesthetic ideas from across Europe and the world.

29 *H.M.S. Royal Prince and other vessels at the Four Days Battle, 1–4 June, 1666.* By Abraham Storck. The painting depicts a bloody engagement off the East Anglian coast between English and Dutch ships of the line during the second Anglo-Dutch War of 1665–7, one of three wars that the two countries fought in the seventeenth century for commercial and naval supremacy. Oil on canvas. © National Maritime Museum, London.

30 Printed handkerchief depicting the victories of England and her allies in the War of Spanish Succession, 1707. Lettering engraved by Robert Spofforth. After the Duke of Marlborough's military successes in 1703 and 1704 he began to be portrayed as a hero, his victories celebrated in popular prints, songs and on decorative objects. Silk, printed from an engraved plate. VAM T.85-1934.

ENGLAND OVERSEAS, 1500 AND 1689

John Styles

In 1500 England had no overseas possessions beyond the British Isles, except Calais in France, a short distance across the English Channel. Calais was the last vestige of the vast French territories that the Kings of England had controlled during the later Middle Ages. The Scots, the Welsh and the Irish held no overseas territories. England lost Calais to the French in 1557, but by that date was beginning to participate in the projection of European power and trade into the Americas and Asia, which had begun with the voyages of Christopher Columbus to the West Indies and of Vasco da Gama to India at the end of the fifteenth century. Sir Francis Drake circumnavigated the globe in 1580, but it was not until the early seventeenth century that permanent English settlements were established in the extra-European world. The first such settlement in the Americas was at Jamestown in Virginia in 1607 and others quickly followed, both on the North American mainland and in the West Indies. By 1689 English colonies stretched in a broken line along the eastern seaboard of North America, while Barbados and Jamaica were the most important English possessions in the West Indies. Meanwhile the East India Company, established in 1600, had set up a number of trading posts around the Indian coastline, although it had little success in its efforts to sustain permanent posts in China, Japan and South-East Asia. Scottish attempts in the seventeenth century to establish colonies in the Americas and to open up regular trade with Asia failed.

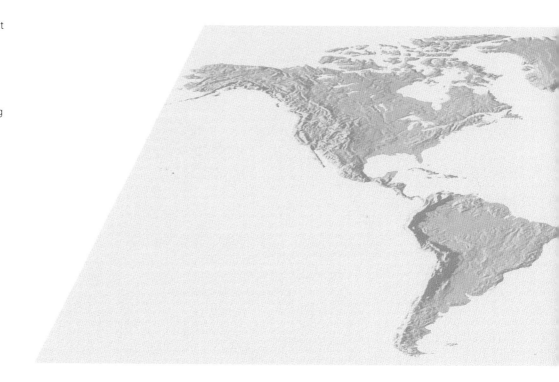

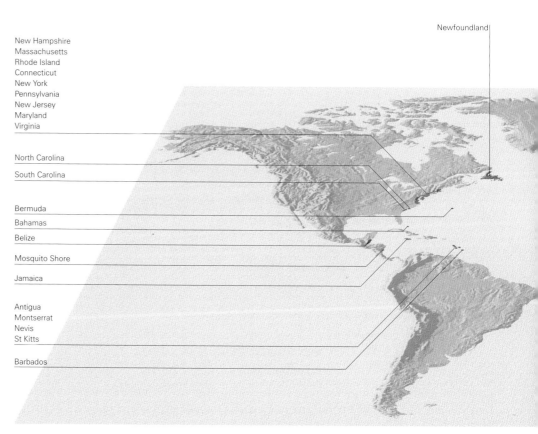

New Hampshire
Massachusetts
Rhode Island
Connecticut
New York
Pennsylvania
New Jersey
Maryland
Virginia

North Carolina

South Carolina

Bermuda

Bahamas

Belize

Mosquito Shore

Jamaica

Antigua
Montserrat
Nevis
St Kitts

Barbados

Newfoundland

Ireland

ENGLAND

Calais

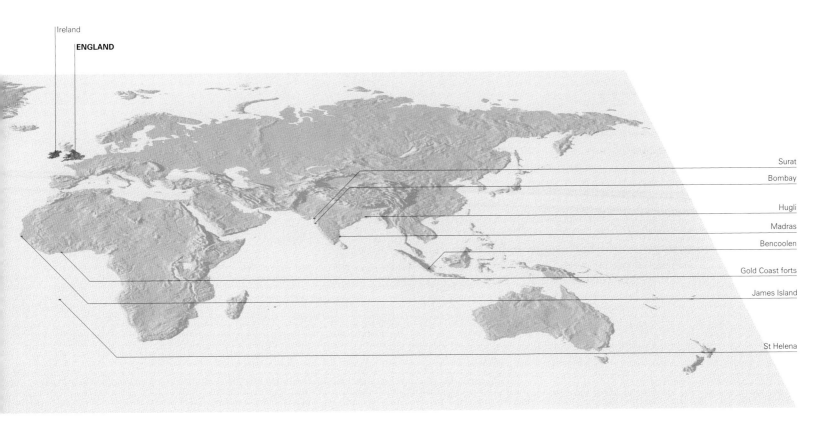

Ireland

ENGLAND

Surat

Bombay

Hugli

Madras

Bencoolen

Gold Coast forts

James Island

St Helena

6. Trade and manufactures

This transformation of design and the decorative arts in Britain owed much to the expansion of trade and manufactures. Britain was one of the principal beneficiaries of the broad shift in the balance of Europe's economy away from the Mediterranean towards the north-western seaboard, between the end of the Middle Ages and the beginning of the eighteenth century, reflecting the rise of Atlantic commerce and global sea routes. This brought stagnation to Venice and Genoa, boom to Amsterdam and London. Nevertheless, it was only in the seventeenth century that the impact of this shift on British commercial life became really marked. Under the Tudors, Britain's trade remained narrowly focused on the Low Countries. Her exports grew, but they continued to consist overwhelmingly of semi-finished woollen cloth. It was craftspeople and merchants in the Low Countries who undertook the immensely skilled and lucrative work of dyeing and finishing the cloth. It was their command of information about international fashion and taste that enabled them to reap the profits of supplying the finished, dyed English cloth to eager customers throughout Europe.

The Low Countries, too, were the source of most of the high-quality manufactured goods that the British imported in growing quantities in return for their cloth throughout the sixteenth century – even when, like Turkish carpets or Italian silks, they originated much further afield. It was principally through the Low Countries that the British became acquainted with Italian silks, lace, glass, tin-glazed ceramics and paper, German swords, armour and textiles, as well as a host of high-design goods made locally, including metalwares, furniture, textiles and leather goods. It is not surprising, therefore, that Netherlandish styles so dominated British design in the period, or that it was in a Netherlandish guise that the stylistic ideas of the Italian Renaissance so often arrived in Britain.

32

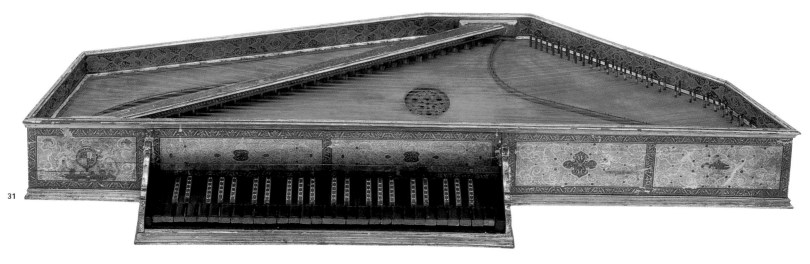

31

31 Spinet, 1570–80. Probably made by Benedictus Florianus in Venice. Possibly commissioned by Elizabeth I and popularly known as 'Queen Elizabeth's virginals'. Cypress case, soundboard and jacks, decorated with parchment, gilding, painting and inlay. VAM 19-1887.

32 Turkish 'Lotto' carpet, about 1550–90. Carpets of this kind are named after the 16th-century Italian artist Lorenzo Lotto, because they appear in some of his paintings. Hand-knotted woollen pile. VAM 903-1897.

It was from the Low Countries, too, that many of the skilled craftspeople came who began to establish the manufacture in Britain of some of the high-design goods previously imported from across the North Sea. Protestant refugees from religious persecution in Antwerp and its hinterland were particularly important in the years after 1560. British-made artefacts replaced more and more European imports, although initially not at the highest levels of the market. The later sixteenth and early seventeenth centuries saw the establishment in London of large-scale production of a wide range of new products, including drinking glasses, tin-glazed ceramics, silk cloth, coaches and watches. Yet the pool of mainly immigrant craftspeople in London, working to the highest international standards of aesthetic and technical quality, remained a small one at the start of the seventeenth century. For its supply of high-design goods, the royal court and other wealthy purchasers continued to depend heavily on imports.

Nevertheless, London was becoming an increasingly important international centre for luxury goods. In the early seventeenth century England began to participate substantially in the new intercontinental trades with Asia and the Americas, which had in the previous century been virtually monopolized by the Portuguese and Spanish. The English East India Company was founded in 1600. The first permanent English settlement in the Americas, at Jamestown in Virginia, was established in 1607. Luxury goods like Indian decorated cottons and Japanese lacquer began to arrive direct from Asia, albeit in small quantities. The playwright Ben Jonson caught the mood in an entertainment that he wrote for the opening of the New Exchange in 1609. A shopboy shouts, 'What doe you lacke? What is't you buy? Veary fine China stuffes, of all kindes and quallityes? China chaynes, China braceletts, China scarfes, China fannes, China girdles, China knives, China boxes, China cabinetts.'

As the seventeenth century progressed, the direct intercontinental trade between London and the Americas and Asia underwent massive growth. It was accompanied by a corresponding acceleration in the pace at which exotic new commodities – tobacco, sugar, coffee, tea, cotton textiles – arrived in the city. By the end of the century the re-export of exotic goods to other parts of Europe had became a significant element of Britain's trade. Britain had become one of the principal gateways through which Europeans secured the products of a wider world.

Otherwise, British exports in the seventeenth century continued to consist predominantly of woollen textiles, but there was a striking change in the kind of cloth being made and in its destination, which signalled the increasing sophistication of British manufacturing and commerce. Trade shifted away from the supply to merchants in the Low Countries of undyed, semi-finished cloth towards the export of a diverse range of lighter, often colourful finished

33 Italian silk fabric, 1600–20. The design and colouring of this silk are very similar to that of the silk used in a dress worn by Queen Anne, wife of James I and VI, as portrayed in a painting by Marcus Gheeraerts the Younger, about 1605–10. Woven silk brocaded with metal thread. VAM T.361-1970.

34 Chinese porcelain ewer with English mounts; ewer 1560–85, mounts with hallmarks for 1585–6. Porcelain was a great rarity at this period and, in common with other decorative curiosities, was often mounted in precious metal. Wanli porcelain and silver-gilt mounts. [h. 25.6cm]. VAM 7915-1862.

35 Jug, about 1620. Made in London, probably in Southwark. Tin-glazed earthenware was made in London from the 1570s, having previously been imported from Italy and the Low Countries. Tin-glazed earthenware, painted in oxide colours. [h. 32.2cm]. VAM C.5-1974.

cloths direct to new markets in Italy, Spain and Portugal. At the same time the process of import substitution begun in the sixteenth century continued. It was assisted by the continuing arrival of foreign craftspeople. They included the Protestant Huguenot refugees, exiled from Catholic France as a result of the Revocation of the Edict of Nantes in 1685, who brought new skills across the whole range of the decorative arts. With the help of these foreigners, London rapidly evolved in the course of the seventeenth century from a city with a manufacturing capacity that was limited, both in the range and the quality of its products, into a centre of production capable of performing in many manufacturing trades to the highest western European standards of technique and aesthetics, approaching the same level as, for example, Paris or Amsterdam. By the end of the Stuart era Britain was manufacturing virtually the whole range of high-design products that the country had previously imported, from stoneware to decorated cotton textiles, although there remained a few notable exceptions, such as porcelain. In addition, Britain had begun to acquire an unprecedented European-wide reputation as a leader in a range of sophisticated manufactures, most notably scientific instruments, clocks and watches.

The international standing of British manufactures at the end of the seventeenth century was summed up by the Swiss visitor Béat-Louis de Muralt. 'English artisans have acquired a great reputation in the world, in many

things with reason; they excel in watchmaking, carpentry, in making saddles and all sorts of tools.' But he also noted their limitations. 'On the whole, in jewellery and all sorts of frivolities more curious than necessary, they are surpassed by the French, and for these things their masters come from Paris.'

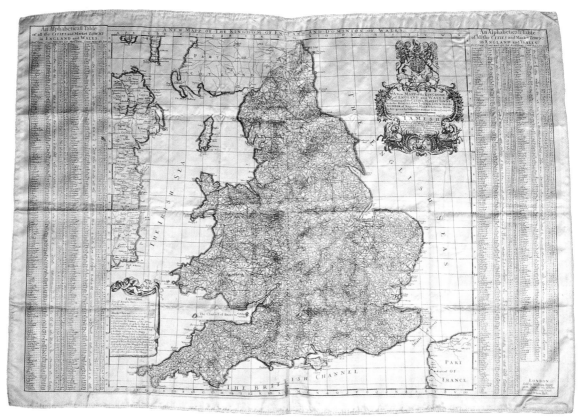

36 Watch and case, about 1700. Made in London by Daniel Quare. Quare invented a repeating mechanism for watches, which was awarded a patent by James II. Engraved silver cases, silver dial; quarter-repeating movement with verge escapement. VAM 1362-1904.

37 *Design for a balustrade and two details for screens*, 1693. Designed by the French Huguenot ironsmith Jean Tijou (active in England 1688–1712). Engraved in London by Michael Vandergucht, a native of Antwerp, Belgium. Plate from *A New Book of Drawings, Invented and Designed by Jean Tijou*, the earliest English publication of designs for ironwork, 1693. Engraving. VAM 25082:9.

39

7. People

Britain was one of the great economic success stories of sixteenth- and seventeenth-century Europe. Trade grew, manufacturing flourished and, crucially in a country that remained predominantly rural, agriculture thrived. The population doubled to about six and a half million in 1700, but by and large the growing number of inhabitants did not outrun the country's capacity to feed itself. Yet British men and women did not benefit equally from the nation's growing prosperity. The numbers of poor and landless multiplied during the period of rapid population growth between 1550 and 1650, when resources shifted towards the better-off. But in the upper echelons of the social pyramid, among those who formed the principal market for high-design goods, the gulf between the few great noble magnates and other, lesser property owners was much less marked in 1700 than it had been in 1500.

The 160 English noble families of 1688 were just as fabulously rich as their 62 predecessors in 1559. Almost all enjoyed incomes of several thousand pounds a year. It was members of the nobility who constituted the core of the royal court. It was they who built prodigy houses on their rural estates and the great London palaces that came to line the Strand under the early Stuarts. It was they who were the leading collectors of antique and continental art and were among the earliest cultural tourists to Italy. But immediately beneath the nobility in the social hierarchy a great deal changed in the course of the sixteenth and seventeenth centuries. The numbers of lesser rural landowners – the gentry – grew faster than the nobility, while in both London and the provinces there were increasing numbers of prosperous merchants, manufacturers and professionals, whose numbers had been very small at the end of the Middle Ages. At the end of the seventeenth century the English nobility remained tiny by continental European standards, but immediately beneath it on the social

40

---

38 Printed handkerchief depicting a map of the road network of England and Wales and listing market towns and days, about 1686–8. By William Berry. The design testifies to the vitality of inland trade in the late 17th century. Silk handkerchiefs printed with non-washable printer's ink were first produced in the 1650s. Silk, printed from an engraved plate. VAM T.223-1931.

39 *Dudley, 3rd Baron North*, about 1630. By an unknown artist. Dudley North was a leading nobleman at the court of James I. Oil on canvas. VAM P.4-1948.

40 Portraits, probably of Henry Holme of Paul Holme, Yorkshire, his wife Dorothy and their two children, 1628. By an unknown artist. Provincial gentry families were often portrayed in this manner, well dressed, but not in the height of fashion. Oil on panel. VAM W.5-1951.

ladder lay the massed ranks of the moderately wealthy, who numbered many tens of thousands. With incomes at the end of the seventeenth century extending upwards from about £100 a year, their wealth might derive from land, trade or the professions. It was these people, above all, who sustained the businesses of that growing multitude of makers producing high-design objects. Already, in his *Description of England* of 1577, the social commentator and clergyman William Harrison noted that knights, gentlemen, merchants and some other wealthy townspeople far exceeded their predecessors in the ownership of luxury goods. According to Harrison, it was not unusual 'to behold generally their great provision of tapestry, Turkey work, pewter, brass, fine linen, and thereto costly cupboards of plate'.

Harrison was also struck by the growing range of decorative objects that was coming to be owned by people still further down the social scale: the group that was known at the time as the 'middling sort'. It consisted of artisans and shopkeepers, as well as the farmers who had profited from rising prices for agricultural produce. Costly household goods like silver plate and decorative woven textiles had, Harrison reported, 'descended yet lower, even unto the inferior artificers and many farmers'. Initially it was the 'middling sort' in London and prosperous parts of south-east England, like Radwinter, Harrison's own Essex village, who enjoyed these material improvements. In the course of the seventeenth century, however, they became much more widely spread across England. Even among the labouring poor, the seventeenth century saw the acquisition of a growing range of colourful clothing fabrics, as well as access to the first of the exotic new commodities from beyond Europe to secure anything resembling a mass market – tobacco.

41 Fragment of a wall painting, 1632. Based on a suite of prints of *The Five Senses*, engraved by Johannes Barra about 1625. Painted for William Sparrow of Park Farm, Hilton, Huntingdonshire. The well-dressed woman depicted here is indulging in the fashionable activity of tobacco-smoking. Painted plaster. VAM W.28-1946.

8. Ideas

This proliferation of material possessions sat uneasily with the dictates of Christian morality. Religion infused every aspect of people's thinking about their world in the sixteenth and seventeenth centuries. There was a powerful and long-standing tradition in Christian thought that disapproved of luxury, overindulgence and wasteful expenditure on superfluities, emphasizing instead charity and the husbanding of God's gifts to mankind. Puritans, in particular, disapproved of anything that might distract attention from God. They preached relentlessly against the sins of covetousness and vanity, pride and envy, so easily aroused by the allure of worldly things, especially those that were beautiful and fashionable. This view found its most complete expression among the Quakers, the extreme (though not strictly Puritan) sect that emerged in the 1650s. Quakers refused to wear the elaborate fashions of the mid-seventeenth century, sometimes burning in public fashionable accessories like ribbons. Their insistence on plainness extended to decorative goods of all kinds. In 1656 the leading Quaker, George Fox, called on 'all you makers of images, and makers of baubles and toys to please the lusts and vanity of people' to repent, 'lest God lay you in the dust with them, and make you like unto them'.

For Protestants, of course, suspicion of ornament was fuelled by the enthusiastic use of the decorative arts by the Counter-Reformation Catholic Church on the continent. Protestants feared the visceral power of beautiful objects to lure the vulnerable into Catholic superstition. Hence the anxieties expressed in 1624 by the diplomat and art collector, Sir Henry Wotton, that 'there may be a lascivious and there may be likewise a superstitious use, both

42 *Thomas Baker*, about 1638. Made in the Roman workshop of Gianlorenzo Bernini. It was unusual at this date for Englishmen, even wealthy ones, to have themselves sculpted by leading Italian artists. Baker was a Suffolk landed gentleman who is believed to have delivered Van Dyck's triple portrait of Charles I to Bernini in Rome and, while there, commissioned this portrait bust of himself. Marble. VAM A.63-1921.

of picture and of sculpture'. Hence the Puritan hostility to Charles I's church reforms of the 1630s. His reforms suggested an almost Catholic conviction that believers could be seduced into reverence and obedience by wrapping the sacred in beautiful things.

It should be emphasized, however, that although Puritans had profound reservations about some aspects of art and culture, particularly religious images and the theatre, these rarely extended to the decorative arts as a whole. Most Protestants accepted the God-given nature of the social hierarchy and its inequality. Even the Quaker Robert Barclay denied in 1678 that 'we intend to destroy the mutual relation that either is betwixt *prince* and *people*, *master* and *servants*, *parents* and *children*'. Most Protestants expected people to own the things that were appropriate to their stations in life. Kings were expected to be magnificent; labourers to be plain. It was extravagance, excess and overindulgence that were disapproved of. And because many Protestants believed that God rewarded those who followed him in this world as well as in the next, it was possible to interpret material well-being, whether displayed by individuals or by the nation as a whole, as the sign of a lively faith and God's providence.

43 Detail of *A Quakers' meeting*, late 17th century. Probably by Egbert van Heemskirk. This painting caricatures the Quakers' plain dress and their unusual forms of religious observance, particularly their practice of allowing women to preach. Oil on canvas. Library of the Religious Society of Friends.

44 *The dole ceremony at Tichborne House, Hampshire*, 1670. By Gillis van Tilborch. The Catholic landed gentleman Sir Henry Tichborne, his family and servants distribute bread to the local poor. The painting presents an idealization of social hierarchy in which the participants know their place and duty, and behave and dress appropriately. Oil on canvas. Tichborne Park, Hampshire.

By the later Stuart years this kind of providential justification for the ownership of fine things was supplemented by more utilitarian, secular arguments. Sometimes these were shocking in their unabashed materialism. In attempting to account for the dizzying growth of British commercial wealth in the later years of the seventeenth century, economic writers began to turn traditional Christian morality on its head. For the tea dealer and journalist John Houghton, the deadly sins could become economic virtues. 'Our high-living is so far from prejudicing the nation, that it enriches it,' he wrote in the early 1680s. 'Those who are guilty of prodigality, pride, vanity, and luxury, do cause more wealth to the kingdom, than loss to their own estates.' The most lyrical exponent of the disturbing new view that individual greed was good for national wealth was, appropriately, the leading developer of London's West End streets and squares, Nicholas Barbon. In 1690 he argued that the economy would prosper if mankind's natural propensity to acquire attractive things was accepted and encouraged:

> The wants of the mind are infinite, man naturally aspires, and as his mind is elevated, his senses grow more refined, and more capable of delight; his desires are inlarged, and his wants increase with his wishes, which is for everything that is rare, can gratifie his senses, adorn his body, and promote the ease, pleasure, and pomp of life.

It was a view that was to haunt debates about design and the decorative arts for the next century.

45 *The Yarmouth Collection*, about 1676–9. Possibly painted by the Dutch artist Peter Gerritsz van Roestraten. Commissioned by the courtier Robert Paston, first Earl of Yarmouth, of Oxnead Hall, Norfolk. The painting depicts part of Paston's spectacular collection of valuable curiosities, several of them with precious-metal mounts, in a manner that juxtaposes symbols of wealth and luxury with those representing vanity and transience. Oil on canvas. Norwich Castle Museum.

CHAPTER 2

Style

MICHAEL SNODIN

1. The Perpendicular Gothic style

The year 1503 saw the start of the most splendid royal building of the early sixteenth century, the chapel of King Henry VII at the east end of Westminster Abbey. Originally intended as a chantry chapel for the King's uncle, Henry VI, it became the burial place of a number of his successors, including his granddaughter Queen Elizabeth I. But what are we to make of the style, or look, that it presents to us? The chapel's architecture, with its wonderful fan-vaulted roof and complex exterior, is the finest surviving expression of the Perpendicular Gothic style. Perpendicular was among the last developments of the Gothic style, which, in various forms, had dominated European architecture since its birth in France in the middle of the twelfth century. However, unlike all other expressions of Gothic in England, it was not a variation on a French model, but a distinctively English development, which in the case of the chapel was designed and put together by English masons. The same cannot be said for the stained glass, which was made by Flemish painters; or for the 107 carved figures of saints, which were also made by craftspeople from the Low Countries.

The most remarkable foreign contribution, however, was the great bronze and marble tomb of Henry and his queen, centred on the altar and completed in about 1518. This was made by the Florentine sculptor Pietro Torrigiani, a pupil – with Michelangelo (whose nose he broke fighting) – of the Florentine painter Domenico Ghirlandaio. Now we might have expected an Italian sculptor to produce a work in the classically based Italian Renaissance style, which was sweeping up through northern Europe during these very years. We can certainly find Renaissance elements in the putti, figures and ornaments of the sarcophagus, as well as in the human realism of King and Queen, but there, interestingly, it stops. Taken all in all, the tomb, with its reclining figures and Perpendicular-style bronze screen, is a reflection of the Gothic style.

2

1 The Chapel of Henry VII, Westminster Abbey, London, completed 1519.

2 The tomb of Henry VII and Elizabeth of York, Westminster Abbey, London. Made by Pietro Torrigiani and completed about 1518.

2. Mixtures and changes

The stylistic mix presented by Henry VII's chapel, with its foreign and local contributions, was characteristic of much of the story of style in British design and architecture over the next 200 years. In one sense that story was already an old one, for style and design in Britain continued to reflect, as before, new ideas from continental Europe, while the flow of imported goods from abroad not only continued but increased. Thus the Tudor 'antique' work of the period of Henry VIII was dependent on Italian early Renaissance design ideas; the Elizabethan and Jacobean styles on Italian High Renaissance architectural ideas and Mannerist decorative motifs from the Low Countries; and the style of the period of Charles II and William and Mary at the end of the seventeenth century on baroque motifs from France and Holland. In another sense, however, the story was crucially different, for the two centuries from 1500 saw, for the first time, the emergence of peculiarly British varieties of style and design in which local interpretations of foreign styles displayed a new individuality and followed their own paths.

What do we mean when we talk about the style of an object? Style in the widest sense is the 'look' of something – what makes it different from other things. That 'look' has something to do with its shape (or shapes, and how they are handled), its texture and colour, or what we might now call its design.

It is also to do with its decoration, or ornamentation. In the sixteenth and seventeenth centuries ornamentation was the main element in design and the chief indicator of style. Changes in ornament are therefore the main subject of this chapter.

The rapid changes in style that we see today, as in the ebb and flow of modern fashion, might suggest that such shifts are the result of mere whim. In fact, they are usually linked to outside forces: social, ideological and economic. What happened to style in Britain between about 1500 and 1700 was no exception, and a number of major trends can be identified. Firstly, objects made in identifiable styles became available to increasing numbers of people, reflecting the gradual advance of surplus money across British society. The wooden platters, few pots and single rough chair in a typical yeoman farmer's house of about 1500 would probably not have carried any decorative motifs, but the joined furniture, pewter, ceramics and possibly even silver in such a house in 1700 would all have reflected particular styles. In addition, the house itself would probably have shown at least some of the architectural ideas visible in the great house up the road.

Secondly, over this period there was a marked increase in types of styled object, from forks to armchairs, as social etiquette (and its architectural setting) became more complex and domestic comfort increased. Matching this last

3

3 Swakeleys, Hillingdon, London, built
1629–38 for Edmund Wright. The house
is in the 'Artisan Mannerist' style,
combining several foreign influences.

trend was a move, towards the end of the seventeenth century, for the same style to be carried across objects of all types, from wallpapers to ceramics, reflecting French ideas of the totally designed interior.

Thirdly, not only were novel types of objects in demand, but the styles of these objects, and the interiors in which they were used, had to reflect the desires and social aspirations of the new consumers. At the start of the Tudor and Stuart period these styles were not the same all over Britain. In architecture, Scotland, England and Wales were distinct, while in England itself there were wide regional variations. By 1700, however, national styles had emerged, in architecture, interior decoration and movable objects, to which large numbers of consumers aspired.

5

3. Renaissance styles and the persistence of Gothic

It was not until the later 1520s that the Italian Renaissance elements first seen in the royal environment of Henry VII's chapel began to reach beyond court circles. Even then they by no means swept the board, as recognizably Gothic forms and ornamental motifs remained in use long after that date, both on their own and combined with Renaissance ideas. It is also possible to see the persistence of Gothic habits of design in the broader sense, not only in the continuing love of botanical ornament and grotesque human and animal forms, but in a persistent interest, especially up to about 1620, in dense masses of confused ornament.

Such stylistic conservatism is perhaps unexpected in the context of the boom in building and the consumption of goods after about 1570. Thus we find the linenfold panelling typical of the late-Gothic interior in about 1500 in wide use into the second half of the sixteenth century, while the shallow, four-centred arch and characteristic mouldings of Perpendicular Gothic were used in windows and doors well into the seventeenth century and in some areas, like the Cotswolds and northern England, even later. West Country stone buildings offer useful examples, combining Gothic details with simple elevations linked to symmetrical plans ultimately derived from Italian examples. The resulting building type, ideally suited to the smaller manor house,

4

4 Barrington Court, Somerset, built 1552–64, for William Clifton.

5 A cup known as the Howard Grace Cup, with London hallmarks for 1525–6. Mark of a bundle of implements. The bands of ornament are in the Renaissance style, but the cresting on the foot is Gothic. Turned elephant ivory bowl with silver-gilt mounts, set with gemstones and pearls. [h. 27.3cm]. VAM M.2680-1931.

'RENAISSANCE': CLASSICAL OR GOTHIC?

Maurice Howard

In Britain the new interest in the classical past emanating from Italy was first shown in experimentation with forms of ornament. The potential for new decorative ideas was understood long before there was a full grasp of the abstract principles of symmetry and decorum that underlay classical design. The term 'Renaissance' was not used by contemporaries in connection with this ornament, but rather the terms 'antique', 'all'antica' or 'antiques of the latest fashion'. Its formal visual vocabulary included piled-up candelabrum forms, shaped and sculpted into the new invention of the baluster, along with naked cherubs, exotic birds, military trophies, and floral and leaf ornament, especially the acanthus.

The new forms became the starting point for invention and fantasy. Wherever it first appeared, Italian ornament was squashed into irregularly shaped spaces and used alongside local forms. So the 'antique' is found cheek-by-jowl with Gothic tracery and the ogee arch. At first craftspeople in England seemed able to use new forms in a flat and decorative manner, but without restraint or any sense of the need for appropriate mouldings. This first phase was governed by the assumption that ornament had to be lavishly applied or, for small portable objects, made in highly expensive materials. Buildings of traditional design, as well as some tombs and church screens, were covered in all'antica ornament made in terracotta cast from moulds so that it could be replicated as much as possible. Small-scale luxury items met the demands of both courtier and merchant patrons.

6. Screen in the Bedingfield chantry chapel, St John the Evangelist, Oxburgh, Norfolk, about 1525–30. Moulded terracotta.

The language of the antique, particularly the use of column and pilaster, was used as a natural framing device in these smaller items, notably the frontispieces of books, medals, seals and small, engraved implements in gold. There was a growing awareness that the more restrained the ornament, the more dignified was its supportive role for heraldry – then the most significant message of lavish decoration. Equally contributive to the richness of new ornament at this time were motifs originating not from Italy but from the Islamic world. The 'moresque', which was associated with the Moors of North Africa who had only recently been expelled from Spain, provided a different means of covering the decorative field, with complex interlaced and knot patterns.

7. Fragment of a frieze, 1518–22. Made in London. From Suffolk Place, Southwark, London, the house of Charles Brandon, Duke of Suffolk. Terracotta. VAM A.28-1938.

8. Candle snuffers, 1547–53. Made for the Privy Council of Edward VI. Silver-gilt. VAM M.837-1928.

9. Bedpost, about 1520. Oak.
[h. 184.5cm]. VAM W.4A-1920.

10. Portion of panelling, about 1520–30. Photographed about 1899. Probably formed part of the decoration of the Abbey-house at Waltham Abbey, Essex. Oak. [h. 63.4cm]. VAM 2011-1899.

11. Stained glass showing the arms of the Piggott family, 1562. Clear, flashed and pot-metal glass painted with yellow stain and brown enamel. [h. 62cm]. VAM C.126-1929.

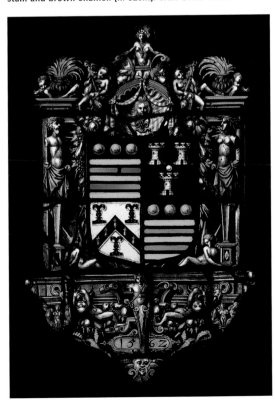

12. Detail of a valance from a bed, with moresque ornament, mid-16th century. Embroidered, velvet with gold thread. [h. 137.2cm]. VAM 4513-1858.

Bellin, an Italian sculptor who had also worked in France. Royal portraits contained Renaissance elements taken from illustrations in architectural books, which also supplied designs for actual ceilings. In Scotland dynastic alliances with France (King James V married two French princesses in succession) led to the French Renaissance façade of Falkland Palace, erected by French masons from 1539.

In England, in the 1540s, other French court models were being emulated. Although all such royal interiors have been lost, drawings show that they were related in design to those at Francis I's palace at Fontainebleau, which used thick, belt-like sculptural elements in a decorative form now known as strapwork. This was to dominate advanced design in Britain for the next 50 years or more, but its main source was not to be the example of the French court but innumerable printed designs coming out of Antwerp.

A little later than 'antique' work, another imported form of ornament arrived in Britain. Called the moresque, after the Muslim Moors of North Africa, it was itself an Italian adaptation of interlaced decorative patterns from the eastern Mediterranean. It was used especially for black-and-white embroidery on clothing; indeed, the first ever pattern book of designs to be

remained fashionable into the early years of the eighteenth century. In Scotland, meanwhile, a Gothic tradition of building, combined with ideas brought directly from French manor houses and châteaux, created a distinct 'Scottish Baronial' style.

By the same token, half-timbered buildings – which, with their elaborate and striking black-and-white pattern effects in wood and plaster, we now think of as typically Tudor – owed nothing (except sometimes their carved details) to ideas from abroad, but were developed from earlier medieval forms of house building. What made them typical products of the Tudor (and Jacobean) age was their extravagance of effect and delight in elaboration, reflecting the desire of their builders to show off their new-found wealth.

In English court circles Renaissance decorative elements were part of a battle for splendour, in which courts all over Europe took part, taking their lead from France (which had itself invaded Italy). Thus at the Field of Cloth of Gold, in 1520, the camps of King Henry VIII and the French King, Francis I, displayed a true unity of style in their Italian tents and temporary palaces (*see 3:10*). The painter Hans Holbein the Younger, brought to England twice by Henry VIII (in 1526 and from 1532), designed jewellery, silver and other precious objects in a German version of the Italian style. The exterior walls of Henry's palace of Nonsuch were sheathed in a dazzling system of painted stucco reliefs of classical figures and carved slate ornament made by Nicholas

13 Craigievar Castle, Grampian region, built 1610–26 for William Forbes. French angle turrets with conical roofs and gables combine with the Scottish tower-house form.

14 *Design for moresque ornament.* 1548. From *Morysse and Damashin renewed and encreased Very profitable for Goldsmythes and Embroderars* by Thomas Geminus. Engraving. VAM 19009.

published in England was a book of moresques aimed at embroiderers and goldsmiths. The book was put out in 1548 by Thomas Geminus, an artist from France, who had arrived in England in about 1540. Moresque became the chief ornament on the standard model of communion cup developed after the Reformation. Copied from secular drinking cups from Germany and Flanders, these were very different from the chalices of the Catholic Church, from whose melted silver they were made, and a rare instance of the new Renaissance style being used as a signal of change and reform.

15 *Design for an interior*, about 1545. Intended for Henry VIII, perhaps for Whitehall Palace, London. The figures and strapwork are very similar to work carried out for King Francis I at Fontainebleau: it is drawn in the French style and may show work to be carried out by French craftspeople. Pen and ink. Musée du Louvre.

4. Going classical

The years around 1550 saw the beginnings of a greater interest in the true nature of classical design in architecture, with its emphasis on proportion, symmetry and balance, and the systematic use of the classical orders. In 1550 the Duke of Northumberland sent John Shute, a painter and member of his household, to Rome to 'confer with the doings of the skilful masters in architecture, and also to view such ancient monuments thereof as are still extant'. In 1563 Shute published the *First and Chief Grounds of Architecture*, the first architectural book in English. It was but a weak reflection of what might have been. A slim volume, published too late, it was largely derived from other architectural works, especially those of the Italian architect Sebastiano Serlio, whose illustrated architectural publications, put out between 1537 and 1551, were among the most influential in Europe.

By contrast, direct experience of contemporary French classical building was probably the chief spur behind the design of Somerset House in London, built from 1547. Although composed in a traditional Tudor Gothic manner, its façade on the Strand (made of stone rather than brick) was the first classically proportioned symmetrical structure in England (*see 3:23*). Its pedimented windows were arranged symmetrically and not according to internal needs. At the centre was a gatehouse based on a Roman triumphal arch, with the classical orders correctly disposed. The general flavour, however, was French.

For all its pioneering elements, Somerset House was a rather unsatisfactory composition. Longleat in Wiltshire, one of the earliest of the great 'prodigy houses' built by the nobles and new magnates of the Elizabethan and Jacobean period, is by contrast a masterpiece of symmetry, balance and control, with its four glittering façades – at least half glass – all turned outwards.

16

16 View of Longleat House, Wiltshire, 1678. By Jan Siberechts. The house was built in 1567–80, incorporating work from 1554 for Sir John Thynne, with the masons Robert Smythson and Allan Maynard. Oil on canvas. Government Art Collection.

17

Longleat was the first great house to abandon the inward-turning courtyard plan for something recognizably modern. With its sparse French-style ornament, it was a model of restraint compared with later prodigy houses like Burghley, near Stamford (begun in 1575), and Wollaton Hall in Nottinghamshire (begun in 1580). These displayed outside, and more especially inside, a delight in densely applied integrated ornament that was unparalleled up to the nineteenth century (which, interestingly enough, saw an intense revival of interest in the 'Elizabethan' style), with the aim of producing maximum splendour.

18

5. Flemish Mannerism

At Wollaton, a plan taken from Serlio was combined with a mass of crestings, turrets and applied ornament that are classical in detail. Taken together, they nevertheless manage to suggest a castle out of an Arthurian romance, matching the chivalric mood of Queen Elizabeth's court. The idea of massed and confused ornament was, however, not in itself some sort of revival of medieval forms, for this approach to design was a characteristic of the Mannerist style sweeping northern Europe, driven by the designers and architects of Antwerp, then its commercial centre.

In Britain Mannerism not only found its way on to and into prodigy houses, but could just as easily be used for silver, jewellery, textiles, carved woodwork, moulded plaster, book title-pages, church monuments and even garden design. Indeed, the earliest surviving appearance of the style in England was in silver, in a ewer made in 1554, probably by one of the many Flemish craftspeople at work in London; similar ewers, made in Flanders, were in the royal collection by 1550. The style continued in many fields, including architecture, in a progressively simplified form, up to the 1620s; and in furniture made in the north of England even longer.

---

17 The east front of Wollaton Hall, Nottinghamshire, built 1580–8. Designed by Robert Smythson for Sir Francis Willoughby.

18 The Wyndham ewer, with London hallmarks for 1554–5. Mark of intersecting triangles. Silver gilt. [h. 35cm]. The British Museum.

JACOBEAN EXTRAVAGANCE

Maurice Howard

Well-established, inherited stylistic conventions dominated royal patronage during the early years of the Jacobean court. On the accession of James VI of Scotland to the throne of England, as James I in 1603, his consort, Anne of Denmark, inherited the vast wardrobe of Elizabeth I. Court fashions, especially the French farthingale for women's dress, remained unchanged for more than 15 years, probably because of this legacy. In buildings, the lead was at first taken by great courtiers rather than by the Crown. In 1607 James forced the swap of the old royal palace of Hatfield for the most glamorous of all late-Elizabethan courtier houses, Lord Burghley's Theobalds in Hertfordshire.

This dependence on the Elizabethan past, but regrouped to create ever-richer effects, is reflected throughout the decorative arts of the period. The great pattern books of the 1580s and 1590s, especially those of the German Wendel Dietterlin and the Netherlander Hans Vredeman de Vries, remained major source books. In architecture, work on churches, civic buildings, country houses and the colleges at Oxford and Cambridge often concentrated the most elaborate effects on entrance porches, where the classical orders were multiplied and stacked on top of each other to frame the heraldry of either individuals or institutions.

In his portraits, Richard Sackville, the third Earl of Dorset, exhibited his lifestyle and his patronage, both key features of contemporary extravagance. He continued the great schemes of decoration and furnishing begun by his grandfather, the first Earl, at the family seat of Knole in Kent. He spent enormous sums in London, a magnet for all aspiring young courtiers, where, as his wife noted in her diary, 'He went much abroad to Cocking, to Bowling Alleys, to Plays and Horse Races.' He dressed lavishly to match, as recorded in the more than 100 items in his wardrobe inventoried in 1617, the year after his death.

The last decade of James's reign, after about 1615, was to see significant changes in fashion, as discerning and well-travelled patrons like the second (Howard) Earl of Arundel and the first Duke of Buckingham shaped new tastes in collecting and commissioning painting. And the work of Inigo Jones, with his scrupulous examination of Italian classical and Renaissance architecture, initiated a new phase in the country's absorption of foreign styles of building.

19. The loggia at Hatfield House, Hertfordshire, about 1611. Possibly designed by Inigo Jones for Robert Cecil, first Earl of Salisbury.

20. Reproduction of a ewer in the form of a leopard of 1600–1, made for Queen Elizabeth I; the original in the Kremlin, Moscow. Made by Elkington's of Birmingham in 1884. Electrotype. [h. 93cm]. VAM M.51-1996.

22. The great staircase at Knole, Kent, 1605–8. Made for Thomas Sackville, first Earl of Dorset. Probably painted by Paul Isaacson. The paintings represent the Ages of Man and the Virtues. They and the ornament are adapted from Flemish prints.

21. *Richard Sackville, third Earl of Dorset*, 1616. By Isaac Oliver. Watercolour on vellum, stuck to card. VAM 721-1882.

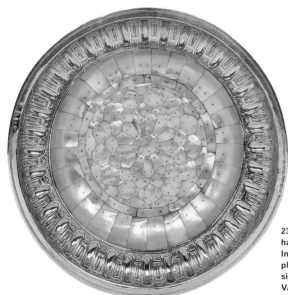

23. Bowl, with London hallmarks for 1621–2. Indian mother-of-pearl plaques, mounted in silver-gilt. [diam. 33.9cm]. VAM M.17-1968.

24. Basin, with London hallmarks for 1607–8. Sponsor's mark 'RS' over a device in a plain shield. Silver-gilt. [diam. 56.7cm]. VAM M.6-1961.

25

The essential elements of the Mannerist style were strapwork and the moresque, combined with the classical grotesque – a framework of plants and fantastic and other creatures derived from ancient Roman wall paintings. The grotesque had re-emerged as a decorative device in Rome in about 1500, with the discovery of these paintings, and was further developed by Raphael and his school in the decorations of the Vatican in the 1520s. It became the basis of most European flat decoration up to the start of the nineteenth century. The heavy strapwork grotesques of Fontainebleau were developed in Antwerp in the 1540s into a dense, all-over system of real or fictive three-dimensional ornament of immense versatility. While many of the craftspeople and decorators using this complex style came from abroad, the real secret of its widespread use in Britain, especially in architecture and interior decoration, lay in the fact that it was frequently copied or adapted from the prints of ornament that were pouring out of Antwerp.

The Antwerp style brought with it the notion that architectural treatments could be applied to objects other than architecture. This can be seen especially clearly in furniture, particularly large fixed pieces like beds and court cupboards. In silver, salts were architecturally treated, and classical obelisk finials marked out a distinct group of vessels now known as 'steeple' cups, created to make an effect on architecturally designed dining-room buffets (*see 5:70*).

By the same token, a unified style was brought to the decoration of rooms through the introduction of classical architectural elements. The Bromley by Bow room (from the 'Old Palace' at Bromley by Bow, London, and now in the Victoria and Albert Museum), created in about 1606, is typical, with its panelling set off by decorated pilasters – all, however, put in the shade by the dominating chimneypiece and elaborate plaster ceiling. Such architectural elements would also have been echoed in the motifs found on tapestries and hanging painted cloths that gave these rooms warmth. At Hardwick Hall in Derbyshire are tapestries dating from before 1591 specially woven to size in Flanders to fit above the panelling that was characteristic of the English interior, reminding us that many objects in the new style must have been imported.

The rich density of ornament that characterized strapwork was typical of the whole approach to style around 1600. The same density characterized the flat patterns of fruit and flowers in sprigs and continuous foliage that continued to be popular into the eighteenth century. Although this botanical ornament absorbed from time to time ideas from the mainstream of European ornament, it never quite threw off a love of detail over proportion, which sometimes gave it the naïve quality of folk art. This was probably a true reflection of its use on objects that were at one remove from the highest status, including painted cloths, wall paintings, carved or painted oak, delftware, pewter, beadwork and, above all, embroidered and other worked textiles, the last of which were often made by amateurs following printed and other patterns.

We know very little of how people regarded these new styles, or indeed of attitudes to style in general, although old-fashioned styles were sometimes used to convey traditionalist meanings. Inventories, such as those listing silver, show clerks abandoning the catch-all 'antique work' (for the earlier Renaissance style) and noting down 'crotiske' (grotesque work), personages, marine subjects or snails in their efforts to encompass the complexities of Flemish Mannerism. Far more attention was devoted to recording coats of arms, reflecting the general interest in signs, symbols, emblems and complex devices that dominated European culture. This stimulated the incorporation into Mannerist ornament of allegorical and other figures and figurative scenes on surfaces of all kinds, from silver to wall painting. Such scenes formed part of a complex programme of meaning that was intended to be consciously 'read' by the visitor.

25 Panel, about 1590–1610. With strapwork in the form of a grotesque, this is similar to a design by Hans Vredeman de Vries, published in *Exercitatio Alphabetica Nova et Utilissima*, Antwerp, 1569. The arms are of the Moule family of Northampton and the Hawkins family of Rushall, Staffordshire. Carved and painted oak, the paint not original. VAM 404-1872.

26 Part of a room, 1606. From the 'Old Palace' at Bromley by Bow, London. Oak, limestone and plaster. VAM 248-1894.

26

27 Woman's jacket. Made about 1610, altered about 1620. Worn by Margaret Laton, wife of Francis Laton, Master Yeoman of the Jewel House during the reigns of James I and VI, Charles I and Charles II (*see 4:41*). The embroidered design is taken from printed pattern books and herbals, but was probably by a professional embroiderer. Linen, embroidered with silver and silver-gilt thread, coloured silks, sequins, bobbin lace and spangles. VAM T.228-1994.

27

28

28 Spice bowl, with London hallmarks for 1573–4. Mark of RF, possibly for Roger Flynt. From a set of dessert plates engraved with scenes from the story of Abraham. This one, 'The Triumph of Isaac', was taken from a print in the engraved set *The Triumph of Patience*, 1559, by Maarten van Heemskerk. The borders were copied from other prints. Engraved silver-gilt. VAM M55:B-1946.

'THE GREAT BED OF WARE'

Maurice Howard

29. The Great Bed of Ware, about 1590–1600. Oak, carved and originally painted, with panels of marquetry; modern textile hangings. [h. 267cm]. VAM W.47-1931.

This celebrated bed takes its name from the town of Ware in Hertfordshire. It was perhaps made for a country house, but more probably for one of the great inns at Ware, a busy staging post on the north road out of London. By 1596, when it was adorning such an inn, it was famous enough to be mentioned by a German visitor to England, while Shakespeare refers to it in *Twelfth Night*, which was first performed in 1601. The bed, twice the size of any other great bed of the period, is rumoured to have slept half a dozen couples, yet it shares both form and decoration with more normal beds of the period.

Unlike today, beds were highly prized. They were the site of some of the most significant events of people's lives, often made to celebrate a marriage, accompanied by the ritualistic but ribald ceremony of 'bedding' the newly-weds. Childbirth, too, was attended by celebrative ritual. Among the upper classes, witnesses at the birth were a necessary proof of legitimacy. At the close of life, to die with dignity and appropriate leave-taking in your own bed afforded a welcome degree of control over death. In the royal palaces, distinguished foreign visitors would be shown beds in which kings and queens had died.

The style and content of the decoration of beds was therefore of great significance. Their overall architectural form and decorative elements were taken from the repertoire of Flemish Mannerism. Their carving, inlay and colour combined to give them an exceptional richness and ritualistic significance. Originally richly painted (although only traces now remain), the bed of Ware would also have been lavishly dressed with hangings. When closed, these created a room within the greater room, with the corners of the bed, half-concealed, half-revealed, forming the boundary between public and private worlds.

The foreposts of the bed of Ware are virtuoso pieces of woodcarving from which decorated columns rise up to support the tester. At the other end, the corners of the headboard display satyrs: half-human, half-animal forms surmounting mask-like heads, indicating the potential for sexual pleasure and procreation.

On the bedhead itself, one female and two male terminal figures frame panels of marquetry inlay with perspective scenes of fantastical architecture, derived from prints after the Netherlandish designer, Hans Vredeman de Vries.

30. *The Life and Death of Sir Henry Unton* (detail), **about 1596. By an anonymous artist. Oil on panel. National Portrait Gallery, London.**

31. Detail of the headboard of the Great Bed of Ware, about 1590–1600. The marquetry decoration derived from engravings after designs by Hans Vredeman de Vries.

32. Satyr figure on the Great Bed of Ware, about 1590–1600.

6. Inigo Jones and the revival of classicism

With few exceptions, the buildings and artefacts we have discussed so far used the ancient classical orders and ornament as a decorative device, a glorious mix-and-match, in their striving for maximum splendour. The idea that such classical elements were part of a system dependent on balance and proportion was of course well known, but was either ignored or adapted to fit local customs. It is against this background that we must see the architectural and stylistic innovations of Inigo Jones. The first British architect and designer of international significance in our story so far, his life and career are more fully described in Chapter 3. Jones's two trips to Italy (before 1603 and in 1613–14) enabled him to experience Italian architecture at first hand, notably that of his hero, the sixteenth-century architect Andrea Palladio.

Placed in charge of the royal buildings from 1615, Jones immediately started designing and erecting buildings that showed a profound understanding of the principles of classical architecture. For the first time in Britain, buildings were designed from the ground up, as unified three-dimensional compositions, their plans and exteriors properly coordinated. The earliest of these was the Queen's House at Greenwich, begun in 1616 but not completed until the 1630s (*see 1:19*). The second, the Banqueting House at the Palace of Whitehall, was built in 1619–22. Even in its earliest form, the Queen's House, at Greenwich, with its unadorned walls and carefully spaced windows, was startlingly plain – we need only compare it with Charlton House nearby, built a little earlier.

34

In fact contemporary commentators failed to spot its revolutionary aesthetic qualities, one describing the Queen's House as 'some curious device of Inigo Jones' – in other words, one of those occasional buildings (like the earlier Lyveden New Bield in Northamptonshire) that was intended to convey hidden messages through their odd design.

The Banqueting House, which today hardly draws a glance embedded in the rather monotonous classical grandeur of Whitehall, was equally revolutionary. For the first time the façade of a complete building was controlled by correctly composed, superimposed classical orders. It was developed from a *palazzo* design by Palladio. The interior was no less remarkable. The single room, a vast galleried hall in the proportions of a double cube, like the basilica form advocated by Palladio following the ancient Roman architect Vitruvius, was the first great classical space to be made in Britain (*see 3:40*).

33

33 The west front of Charlton House, Greenwich, London, built 1607–12 for Sir Adam Newton, tutor to Henry, Prince of Wales.

34 The Banqueting House, Whitehall, London, built 1619–22. Designed by Inigo Jones.

During Jones's lifetime (he died in 1652) his style was very largely restricted to the court and its circles. However, in the theatre and its close relation, interior decoration, Jones's work for the court had a major national effect. For these areas he developed a style that combined ideas from late sixteenth-century Italy and mid-sixteenth-century France, the latter taken largely from prints. After the arrival in 1625 of Henrietta Maria, daughter of the King of France, a significant modern French element was imported, not only in the form of artists and craftspeople, but in terms of style. Interiors took on elements, often very literally translated, from the early baroque style that was emerging in France on the back of ideas from Italy. While very few such interiors by Jones survive, the work of his pupil John Webb is instructive. For the famous double-cube room at Wilton House near Salisbury, made in 1649, Webb designed a space richly French in style, with panelled walls and a deeply coved ceiling painted with figure scenes and swags of flowers and fruit, all to become major themes over the next 50 years.

35

36

35 *Design for a chimneypiece at the Queen's House, Greenwich*, London, 1636. Designed by Inigo Jones in the French style. Pen and ink. RIBA Library Drawings Collection.

36 The double-cube room, Wilton House, Wiltshire, made about 1649. Designed by John Webb. The ceiling cove painted by Edward Pierce.

A good idea of the French-influenced court style of the 1630s at a slightly more modest level is to be obtained at Ham House, London, decorated for William Murray, Gentleman of the Bedchamber to Charles I and first Earl of Dysart, with its French ceremonial staircase (one of the first in England) and its painted decoration by Franz Cleyn from Germany. Cleyn also designed furniture carrying Jones's characteristic mask motifs, and the tapestries for the London tapestry works at Mortlake, founded in 1619. The tapestries and Cleyn's own ornament prints show the same type of smoothed-out grotesque ornament as at Ham, and reflect the fleshy, fat cartouches characteristic of the auricular style, which began in Holland in about 1600 and was named after its resemblance to the forms of the ear. This style was especially promoted by the van Vianen goldsmithing family of Utrecht, one of whose members, Christiaen, came to London in about 1630 to work for Charles I and returned in 1660. The auricular style continued to be popular until after 1660, becoming incorporated into mainstream baroque botanical ornament, especially in carving in both stone (church monuments) and wood, notably in the so-called 'Sunderland' picture-frame type.

By the 1650s the French-style elements of the Jonesian interiors had spread well beyond court level to gentry houses far from London, no doubt aided by a set of prints first published by Cleyn and the painter Edward Pierce the Elder (who had worked for Jones) in 1640. This combined style was, however, most clearly shown in the work of immigrant artists, such as the tomb of the Duke of Buckingham in Westminster Abbey, carved by Isaac Besnier, with bronze work by the sculptor Hubert le Sueur.

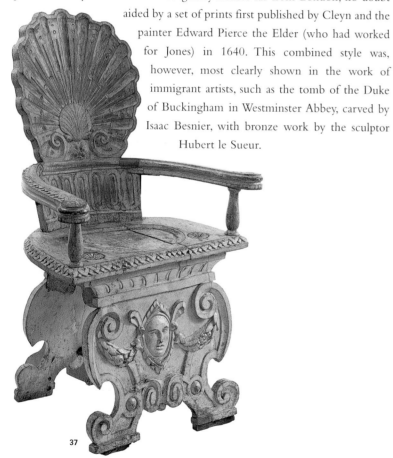

37 Chair, about 1625. Possibly designed by Francis Cleyn. The design is based on Italian models. Carved oak and beech, with traces of gilding. VAM W9-1953.

38 Standish (inkstand), with London hallmarks for 1639–40. Mark of AI, possibly for Alexander Jackson. Probably made in the London workshop of Christiaen van Vianen. Silver. VAM Anonymous loan.

7. 'Artisan Mannerism'

Outside court circles, architecture from the 1620s to the 1640s was experiencing the gradual spread of Mannerism from the great prodigy houses to smaller country houses, and finally to street architecture in towns. But the forms were changing under the impact of new ideas. In London the newest buildings were of brick and were more regular and symmetrical in their proportions. Both owed much to royal proclamations on building begun by James I and VI, who declared in 1615 'that we found our cities and suburbs of sticks and left them of brick, being a material far more durable, safe from fire and beautiful and magnificent'. The proclamations, administered and devised in detail by Jones and the Commissioners of New Building of the 1630s, ordained specifically classical forms, such as windows taller than they were broad. But in areas without such controls, timber buildings became ever larger and more elaborate and remained Jacobean in style. The new London houses were built with shaped scrolling gables and 'pergulas' (iron balconies), an innovation from Italy, both developments perhaps first introduced by Jones (*see 2:3*).

His influence also lay behind the building of the first English terraced houses, a row in London's Great Queen Street erected in 1637, evidently inspired by his arcaded building at Covent Garden. The giant classical pilasters on their façades were widely copied and can still be found on the front of Lindsey House in Lincoln's Inn Fields, a remarkable survivor of about 1640. The interiors of such houses might contain elements in the Jacobean style mixed with more recent notions.

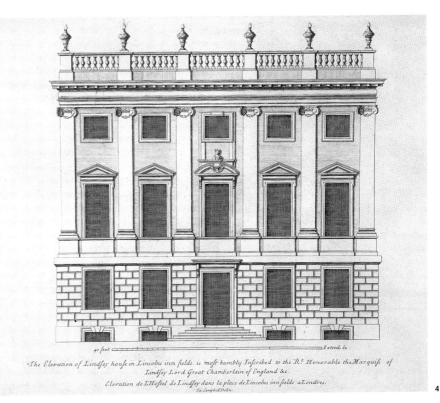

39 The staircase, Ham House, London. Built 1637–8.

40 Design for a frieze, 1668. Copied from a frieze design by Edward Pierce the Elder from a set first published in 1640. Published by Edward Tooker. Engraving. VAM E.3617-1907.

41 *Lindsey House, Lincoln's Inn Fields, London*, built about 1640. Plate from *Vitruvius Britannicus* by Colen Campbell, second edition 1725 (first published 1715). Lindsey House was in 1715 believed to have been designed by Inigo Jones. It was perhaps designed by the sculptor/mason Nicholas Stone, a friend of the owner of the house, Sir David Cunningham. Engraving. VAM 64.H.93.

8. The civil war and Restoration

The political cataclysm of civil war and the period of Puritan rule in the 1640s and 1650s were significant in terms of stylistic developments later in the century, but not in the way one might expect. Such Puritan acts as the demolishing of maypoles, banning of plays and destruction of images in churches were not echoed in architecture or the applied arts, which showed little sign of becoming less elaborate. Indeed, one of the earliest datable examples of the naturalistic acanthus-leaf style, which was to become characteristic of the reign of Charles II, appeared in the carved details of the interior of Thorpe Hall in Northamptonshire, the house of Oliver Cromwell's Chief Justice, a couple of years before the Restoration.

The most significant effect of political events on design was in fact the opening up of Britain to foreign influences through time spent abroad by political exiles and others. These included the architect Roger Pratt, who returned to England after the execution of Charles I to build for his cousin the house of Coleshill in Berkshire. Coleshill was a clever mix of themes from France, Holland, Italy and England, demonstrating the breadth of Pratt's continental experience, as well as contact with Inigo Jones. The result was a serene and balanced classical house of a type that was to have a huge influence on later British architecture, largely through a more accessible house in the same manner, Pratt's Clarendon House in Piccadilly, which was built shortly after the Restoration.

43

42

42 Coleshill, Berkshire, begun after 1649, completed 1662. Designed by Sir Roger Pratt for Sir George Pratt. Burned in 1952 and subsequently demolished.

43 The great parlour door, Thorpe Hall, Northamptonshire, about 1658. Record drawing made about 1730. Thorpe Hall was designed by Peter Mills for Oliver St John, Chief Justice to Oliver Cromwell. Pen and ink. VAM 1833-1885.

9. Restoration baroque

The effects of exile were, of course, most strongly felt after the Restoration in 1660. Most of Charles II's supporters had spent the years of exile in Holland, and the styles of that country, and of France, had a profound effect on design and architecture. The royal architect Hugh May developed, from 1663 onwards, a modest Dutch house type in brick and stone, which was widely imitated and introduced the general use of applied classical orders and central pediments.

Sir Christopher Wren, the most important architect of the second half of the century, began his architectural career in 1662. His chapel at Pembroke College, Cambridge (1663), was the first college chapel to be built without a trace of Gothic. He did not travel abroad until 1665, but then absorbed all he could see. 'I bring you almost all France on paper,' he wrote, and, 'I have purchas'd a great deal of taille-douce [prints] that I might give our countrymen examples of ornaments and grotesks, in which the Italians themselves confess the French excell.' Wren's great architectural opportunity came with the Fire of London of 1666 and the subsequent rebuilding of 52 City churches (largely between 1670 and 1686) and St Paul's Cathedral (completed in 1709), the first large group of classical churches ever to be built in Britain. Indeed, from 1660 correctly detailed classical forms became the architectural norm in Britain and Mannerism was gradually forgotten. This trend was greatly encouraged by the rebuilding after the fire, which was done to new regulations requiring brick construction and adherence to certain proportions and sizes.

The interior details of the new classical buildings were heavily indebted to ideas from Holland and France. From the 1620s a greater interest on the continent in botany and flower painting was matched by the introduction of ever more accurate plants in decoration.

44 Eltham Lodge, Greenwich, London, built 1663–4. Designed by Hugh May for Sir John Shaw, Bt.

45 Lantern clock, about 1650. Signed by the clock- and watchmaker David Bouquet, a French immigrant who had arrived in London by 1628. Engraved silver. VAM M.1139-1926.

THE BAROQUE IN ENGLAND

Tessa Murdoch

As heir to the English throne, Charles II spent 12 years in exile absorbing continental design, which was then developing into the baroque style. On his Restoration in 1660, he embarked on the refurbishment of his royal palaces. The architect Hugh May, who also spent four years in Holland, was responsible for Windsor Castle. The Royal Chapel there, said to be the finest baroque interior in England, was painted by the Italian artist Antonio Verrio in *trompe l'oeil* with twisted columns framing scenes of the Last Supper and Christ healing the sick, below a cloud-filled ceiling depicting the Resurrection. The decorative painting appeared to dissolve the rectilinear structure of the building. In the same way, the dramatic baroque portrait of the monarch by the French sculptor Honoré Pelle invades the viewer's space with its twisted pose and dramatic swirling drapery.

An interest in technical developments promoted the use of characteristic baroque forms. Lathe-turning produced spirally twisted forms in wood, which were used as effective supports for furniture and architectural

47. *Charles II*, 1684. By Honoré Pelle. Carved in Genoa. Marble. [h. 128.9cm]. VAM 239-1881.

woodwork. A general fascination with artistic virtuosity aided the career of the young Dutch-trained carver Grinling Gibbons, who provided naturalistic decoration for both secular and ecclesiastical interiors. Also inspired by continental example, the practice of marquetry, introduced in the 1660s, provided a novel form of decoration for furniture, imitating the Italian use of inlaid hardstones, yet satisfying contemporary interest in the texture of native woods.

In the 1690s the role of court designer became, in imitation of the French example, an important means of ensuring unity of design across interiors. Daniel Marot, designer to William and Mary, guided the production of decorative painting, sculpture, furnishings, upholstery and ceramics. Courtiers swiftly imitated the royal example. In upholstered furniture, richness of colour and texture was impressively combined with new forms. Continental craftspeople settled in Britain, bringing innovative styles and standards of excellence. They were eagerly commissioned by the monarchs, their courtiers, officers of state and military leaders.

46. Musical trophy, about 1692. Designed and carved by Grinling Gibbons, at Petworth House, Sussex. Limewood.

48. Table, the top showing a view of Wingerworth Hall, Derbyshire, about 1674. Made to commemorate the marriage of Sir Henry Hunloke and Katherine Tyrwhitt in 1673/4. Elm and walnut veneer with marquetry of various woods on oak and pine carcase. VAM W.53-1948.

49. Settee, 1690–1700. From Hampton Court, Herefordshire. Walnut legs, the frame upholstered in embroidery of wool and silk, the back and sides covered in glazed wool; cushions lined with kidskin, and silk trimmings. [h. 137.8cm]. VAM W.15-1945.

50. Cabinet, about 1700. Possibly made in London by John Byfield. Made to commemorate the marriage between Margaret Trotter and George Lawson, probably for East Harsley Castle, Yorkshire. Walnut veneer, marquetry of burr walnut, sycamore, holly, pine and oak carcase. [h. 240cm]. VAM W.136-1928.

Baroque architecture became fully developed in the early eighteenth century. Sir Christopher Wren's St Paul's Cathedral was completed in 1710; other London churches included Nicholas Hawksmoor's Christ Church, Spitalfields (1714–29) and James Gibbs's St Martin-in-the-Fields (1722–6). Great houses built for the nobility included the palace-like Castle Howard, described by its architect Sir John Vanbrugh as 'the top seat and garden in England'.

51. The Royal Chapel, Windsor Castle, Berkshire. Designed by Hugh May, the painted decoration by Antonio Verrio, about 1675–84. Watercolour by Charles Wild, 1815–18 © The Royal Collection.

By the 1640s dense, three-dimensional vegetable ornament had become the leading theme in France and was used in a new type of rich but soberly designed interior, ultimately derived from Italian baroque examples. By the 1660s this design approach had become the official French style, in Paris and at Versailles, and was playing a key role in the propaganda for Louis XIV. It was this interior style, which combined botanical (and especially leaf) ornament in plaster and carved wood with figurative wall and ceiling painting showing allegorical or symbolic subjects, that was taken up in Britain in the 1660s in direct emulation of the court of Louis. It is significant that it was at this moment that the London publisher John Overton chose to reissue sets of leaf ornament by Edward Pierce the Elder and others, as well as a copy (in 1672) of a set of acanthus scrolls first published in Italy in the 1620s.

This period saw the height of development of the panelled interior, with rooms commonly being lined with large fielded panels thrust forward on bulbous bolection mouldings. In elaborate schemes such panelling would be set off by deeply undercut naturalistic ornament and three-dimensional figures carried out in a style derived from slightly earlier Dutch and possibly German precedents. The great master of this style, and its chief promoter, was the famous woodcarver and sculptor Grinling Gibbons, whose work matured in the mid-1670s, although there were many others working in the same manner.

The undercut wood was frequently matched by ceilings in which deeply projecting mouldings arranged along Jonesian patterns were embellished with startlingly naturalistic leafage, made possible by the new technique of attaching individual elements in hard plaster. The third decorative element, large-scale illusionistic wall painting, was introduced with the arrival in about 1672 of the Italian painter Antonio Verrio. He was the first of a number of painters, chiefly French and Italian, but including the Englishman Sir James Thornhill, who supplied the need for large allegorical or symbolic wall or ceiling paintings up to the mid-eighteenth century.

The vegetable naturalism seen in interiors from the 1660s was echoed to some extent in the smaller objects of the house; by the 1680s it had developed into a generalized form of scrolling acanthus that was applied to goods of all sorts. In the 1660s it appears to have been strongest in silver embossed with fruit and flowers, perhaps because so many of the earliest surviving pieces in the style were made by immigrant silversmiths; it was also often combined with the auricular style.

At a less luxurious level, the characteristic tulip appeared on delftware and enamelled brass. The deeply undercut naturalism of decorative woodcarving was to be found on pieces integral to the room, such as mirrors, while other items such as bookcases (a new form, perhaps from Holland) matched in their mouldings the acanthus carving on the room's cornices and dado rails (see 5:47). Other types of furniture, notably chairs, had legs in a spiral form taken from French or Dutch precedents. Such baroque-style furniture only became usual in the 1670s, for much furniture of the 1660s still followed the old Flemish Mannerist styles.

52 The State Bedroom, Powis Castle, Powis, about 1668. The furniture from about 1725.

53 Tile from a set probably made for the Water Gallery, Hampton Court Palace, London, about 1694. Made in Delft, the Netherlands, at the 'Greek A' factory and marked with the monogram of its proprietor from 1686 to 1701, Adrianus Kocx. From a design by Daniel Marot. Tin-glazed earthenware, painted in blue (delftware). [h. 61cm]. VAM C.13-1956.

10. Daniel Marot and a new style

While the scrolling acanthus continued to be an underlying ornamental theme, from the 1680s a new style from France began to make itself felt, especially after the accession of William and Mary in 1688. It reflected a revived concentration on the grotesque, notably in the work of the French court designer Jean Berain, who developed a new form of grotesque in which the clear, light strapwork structures were adorned with acanthus and varied figures, animals and other motifs. This type of grotesque not only found its way on to flat decorations, painted panels and textiles, carved mouldings, stamped leathers, wallpapers and even ironwork, but was matched by new forms of vessel and vase design in which clearly expressed mouldings divided up plain but bold shapes. Foreign designers and craftspeople played a central role in the introduction of the style to Britain. One of the key figures was William and Mary's court *dessinateur*, Daniel Marot, a French Huguenot and son of a designer to Louis XIV, who had emigrated to Holland. He was in England between the mid-1690s and about 1700 and is known to have worked for the Queen, laying out the garden at Hampton Court. The Dutch delftware tiles from the Water Gallery at Hampton Court, of about 1694, followed his designs. Other rooms in the Water Gallery were lined in lacquer, mirrors and marble and were filled with massed displays of East Asian porcelain, blue-and-white delftware on brackets, and flower vases and Delft flower-pyramids on the floor. The style now associated with Marot's name spread well beyond the court, notably to a group of noblemen who both built and furnished in an especially French manner.

54 Dish, about 1670–85. Probably made in London. Earthenware, tin- and lead-glaze painted in colours (delftware). [diam. 33.7cm]. VAM C.244-1911.

55 Looking glass, 1665–72. The frame possibly made by a Dutch or Flemish carver in London. Painted with the arms of Gough of Old Fallings Hall and Perry Hall, Staffordshire. Pine wood, carved and decorated with gesso and silver leaf, retaining traces of red glaze, later paint and gilding. [h.176.5cm]. VAM W.37-1949.

Marot helped established the idea of the unified interior, in which the decoration, furnishings and furniture of a room were all designed and supplied at the same time in a coordinated style. While richly decorative, Marot's style was fundamentally rectilinear and architectonic, with a strong tendency towards verticality. Wall areas were clearly divided in long vertical panels and the same Berainesque patterns and grotesques were used on upholstery, furnishings, wall elements and carved furniture details. In areas such as entrance halls the architectonic approach produced interiors of exceptional sculptural power, in which wood and plaster were frequently painted to resemble the stone of the floors. This approach and stylistic unity also encouraged the introduction of coordinated groups of furniture on the French model. The most important was the group of a table and candlestand, often accompanied by a mirror, designed as fixed features of a room. The decorative stylistic unity also extended to the gardens, where plantings and gravel patterns repeated on a grand scale the designs found indoors.

The porcelain displays in Queen Mary's Water Gallery were part of a European-wide craze for goods from the Indies (*see pp. 140–1*). In the porcelain cabinets created from the 1680s onwards, hundreds of pieces were

56 Chair, about 1700. Beech carved, painted and gilded; modern cut-velvet upholstery. The original upholstery was Genoa velvet in red, blue and black on a buff background. VAM W.11-1964.

57 *Design for a state bedroom*, 1702. Reversed copy, probably published in Holland 1712–84, of a plate in the *Second Livre Dappartements* by Daniel Marot (first published 1702). The chimneypiece is decorated with East Asian porcelain. Etching. VAM E.5914-1905.

58 Embroidery, about 1710–20. From a set hung at Stoke Edith, Herefordshire, built in 1697 for Paul Foley, Speaker of the House of Commons. The embroidery may show the garden at Stoke Edith, laid out by George London from 1692. Linen canvas embroidered with silk and wool, with some details in appliqué. VAM T.568-1996.

58

arranged in patterns on classically designed walls. The British interest in blue-and-white was greatly increased by Queen Mary's, whose own particular passion was porcelain. At her palace at Kensington she had 787 pieces of porcelain, 154 of which were in her bedchamber.

Such decorative displays were frequently accommodated on the corner chimneypieces that were characteristic of English interiors. Rooms were also lined in real or imitation lacquer, hung with real or imitation Chinese wallpaper or decorated with tapestries showing Chinese scenes adapted from designs on lacquer and porcelain. Such scenes marked the transition to true chinoiserie – that is, the creation of a distinctly European style based on an evocation of China, in colourful and often playful counterpoint to the high seriousness of the classical baroque.

59

60

59 *Design for a 'Cheminée a Langloise'*, about 1700. By Daniel Marot, from the set *Nouvelles cheminées*. Bolection (stepped) mouldings frame the panels and fireplace opening. The corner setting of the chimney-piece is typically English. Etching. VAM 13857:1.

60 Cabinet on a stand, about 1690–1700. Once the property of Sir Richard Hill. The cabinet has been painted ('japanned') to look like Japanese lacquer. The stand is in the style of Daniel Marot. Stand of carved and silvered pine and lime. VAM W.20-1959.

It was only to be expected that the French influence would also be felt in architecture. At Hampton Court Palace, built in 1690–6, Wren created for William and Mary a scheme that went at least some way towards providing the version of Versailles that all European rulers craved, although in this case with a strongly domestic Dutch feel. More directly French in design were the great houses of some of William and Mary's courtiers, such as Boughton House in Northamptonshire, begun in 1688 for the Duke of Montagu (and Montagu House in London, now demolished), and Petworth in Sussex for the Duke of Somerset. For the east front at Chatsworth in Derbyshire, William Talman designed for the Earl of Devonshire from 1686 a composition that used French

elements such as heavy keystones and a giant order, but treated them in a dramatic and emotional manner. This makes it the first British architectural composition that can be called baroque.

The architectural style first fully introduced at Chatsworth saw its complete development in the years around and immediately after 1700, in a series of exceptional great houses, including Castle Howard in Yorkshire and Blenheim Palace in Oxfordshire. At the former, designed by Sir John Vanbrugh from 1698 for the Earl of Carlisle, a great dome rides for the first time over an English country house. It is a baroque palace fit to match any on the continent. While most of the rooms (where they have survived) show

61 The park front of Hampton Court Palace, London, 1690–6. Designed by Sir Christopher Wren.

62 Castle Howard, North Yorkshire, built 1698–1726. Designed by Sir John Vanbrugh, assisted by Nicholas Hawksmoor, for the Earl of Carlisle.

63 The south front of Chatsworth House, Derbyshire, begun 1686. Designed by William Talman.

themselves as modest exercises in the Marot manner, Castle Howard's hall and flanking paired staircases together form a fantastic piece of baroque spatial design with the feeling of an Italian chapel. Many of the craftspeople were indeed Italian, including the mural painter Giovanni Pellegrini (from Venice) and the first of many Italian-Swiss plasterers to come to Britain, Plura and Giovanni Bagutti.

At Beningbrough Hall nearby, the far less wealthy John Bourchier built from about 1710 another exercise in the baroque. Its exterior is a curious mix of elements taken from Italian pattern books (probably gathered by Bourchier on his Grand Tour) and the interior is almost entirely panelled in wood, with fine Marot-style carving. But the hall and corridors, as at Castle Howard, are grand spatial exercises in plaster and stone.

64

65

64 The hall, Castle Howard, North Yorkshire, created 1709–12. Designed by Sir John Vanbrugh. The chimneypiece probably by Plura and Giovanni Bagutti, the wall painted by Giovanni Antonio Pellegrini, the overdoors by Marco Ricci.

65 Looking through the state apartment from the dressing room at Beningbrough Hall, North Yorkshire, built about 1710–16.

CHAPTER 3

Who led taste?

MICHAEL SNODIN

1. Taste and power

For most people between 1485 and 1714 visual choices were not, as they are today, simply 'a matter of taste', or of changing fashion, available to anyone with the money to indulge them. Fashions did, of course, exist, and changing styles were just as prevalent as they are today. But the business of visual culture, of architecture, design, public displays and the visual arts, existed chiefly to service and reinforce a highly stratified social and political system in which power came from the top. As a result, changes in taste also tended to come from the top. Around 1500 this meant both the Church and the royal court. After the Reformation in the 1530s the court was the dominant authority. Unlike today's monarchy, it was the real centre of government. Henry VIII took a personal lead in royal building and furnishing, while Elizabeth I's political methods and manipulation of her courtiers produced a rich culture of building and furnishing outside the royal palaces, but one that was linked to her person.

By 1700 the court's central influence on taste had weakened noticeably, matching the emergence of the mechanisms of modern government. At one end, courtiers and court officials, like the royal architect Sir Christopher Wren, now took the lead; at the other, the beginning of a recognizably modern system of retail shopping, rapid fashion changes and the spread of visual culture through prints, newspapers and other printed media meant that the visual arts could much more easily be acquired by the new group of high-consuming, more numerous and increasingly important, non-aristocratic 'middling sort' in society.

Maintaining a direct link between social rank and visual culture was essential, especially during a time of increasing wealth. A nobleman could not be more magnificent in his building, furnishing or dress than his sovereign, nor could a servant outdo his master: every rank had its appropriate degree of display. Correspondingly, movement up the social ladder was marked by the acquisition of new, more expensive objects and demotion of the old. In 1577 the commentator William Harrison noted the widespread replacement of wooden plates by pewter ones, which were imitations of those in silver. By 1700 those country yeomen who aspired to the degree of the lesser gentry were sending their pewter to the kitchen and stocking their eating rooms with silver.

Such shifts in consumption were often seen as a threat. Law makers attempted to control inappropriate consumption, not only because of its social effect, but to prevent the import of foreign luxury goods and discourage private luxury on moral grounds. A series of sumptuary laws between 1510 and 1554 set limits on the consumption of luxuries, especially fine clothing, for all except the nobility. Other methods of control were also possible. A subject's over-pretension could, for instance, lead to the confiscation of property, as happened to Cardinal Wolsey and the Duke of Buckingham. Queen Elizabeth, who took great pride in her own magnificent clothes, kept a very sharp eye on those of the ladies at court, on one occasion taking the particularly splendid dress of Lady Mary Howard and trying it on herself. On finding it too short, she said to Lady Mary, '. . . if it become not me as being too short, I am minded it shall never become thee, as being too fine'.

1 *Henry VIII*, 1669. By Remigius van Leemput, derived from a fresco painted by Hans Holbein the Younger at Whitehall Palace, 1537. Henry VIII's portrait reflected not only his worldly power, but also the sumptuous and up-to-date nature of design at court. Oil on canvas. The National Trust, Petworth House.

2

2. How taste travelled

The extent to which changing tastes passed in a 'trickle-down' manner from the court or nobility to other social groups varied greatly and is now often difficult to track. Enterprising craftspeople certainly adapted stylistic court fashions, such as that for Flemish Mannerism, to suit the pockets of burghers and the gentry. Many items were not specially commissioned, but were of standard design and from the start of the Tudor period were available ready-made from a variety of shops and other retailers. In terms of precious metals, before about 1660, it is overwhelmingly this type of lesser object that has survived for our inspection, with only one piece from Elizabeth I's own contributions to her jewel house remaining to give any idea of the splendours that it contained.

The same is true of surviving furniture before about 1660, which consists almost entirely of carved pieces in the Gothic style or more or less crude interpretations of Flemish Mannerism. Only a few pieces, like the famous sea-dog table at Hardwick Hall, which is a French import, survive to give us an idea of the appearance of fine carved furniture at court level, while court-level portrait paintings up to 1650 emphasize instead the luxury world of cloth and comfort, notably the upholstered state chair (no early examples of which survive). Other forms of adaptation as ideas moved down the social scale involved the imitation of expensive objects in cheaper materials. Tapestries were imitated in painted (or 'stained') cloths or replicated as wall paintings, while silver forms were imitated in pewter and ceramics.

3

2 *A very rich Lotterie generall without any Blanckes*, 1567. Advertising sheet by an anonymous artist. While the first prize was a very expensive tapestry, most of the prizes were smaller objects of a standardized type. Woodcut. The Folger Shakespeare Library.

3 Table, made about 1580 in France. Recorded in the inventory of Hardwick Hall, Derbyshire, compiled in 1601. Walnut. The National Trust, Hardwick Hall.

4 *Portrait of an unknown lady*, about 1630. By an unknown English artist. An expensively upholstered chair is prominently displayed. Oil on canvas. VAM 565-1882.

5 Candlestick, dated 1648. Made in Southwark, London, probably at the Pickleherring factory, for William Withers. The design imitates a metal original. Tin-glazed earthenware, painted. VAM 4752-1901.

Attitudes to taste before about 1650, as well as design decisions and processes, are perhaps most clearly shown in the design of buildings. In an age before the emergence of the professional architect, the lead in design was usually taken by the builder himself, in consultation with the mason or other craftsman (often referred to as the 'architect' in contemporary records) who was to erect the building. Typically ideas for the design were gleaned from local and other buildings. In 1603 Henry Percy, Duke of Northumberland, who was planning building works at Syon, wrote that he was 'ready to go, and see Copthall, for now that I am a builder I must borrow of my knowledge somewhat out of Tibbals [Theobalds, Hertfordshire] somewhat out of every place of mark where curiosities are used'.

Sir Robert Townshend, the builder of Raynham Hall in Norfolk, made a tour in 1619, with his mason, of notable English houses, including Hatfield House and Audley End; Townshend even, very exceptionally, took him abroad to the Low Countries. Further down the social scale, John Smythson, from a notable family of surveyors, made careful drawings of Italian 'pergulas' or balconies and other architectural novelties in London in 1619. Builders and, more rarely, masons and surveyors also

7

owned architectural books and prints from which ideas could be drawn: Townshend was reported to have 'many Italian and French books of architecture'. Masons working on several houses carried ideas and personal stylistic mannerisms from job to job. Finally there was the purpose of the building to be considered: show was necessary where social position needed to be maintained; otherwise simple forms sufficed. But the design process was not yet over, for even during building changes could be made.

The results of such a process naturally varied from the conservative to the novel. Raynham reflected the latest London city building styles, as well as incorporating a remarkable Ionic portico closely modelled on the ideas of the royal architect Inigo Jones. In most cases, however, the design process resulted in the emergence of distinctive local and regional styles, which took on the characteristics of court and aristocratic architecture to varying degrees. By 1700 such differences had become minor, marking the emergence of a national architectural style.

6

6 Raynham Hall, Norfolk, begun 1621, finished about 1635.

7 *Bath House and Sir Fulke Greville's house, Holborn, London*, 1619. By John Smythson. Pen, ink and wash. RIBA Library Drawings Collection.

3. The Church

The power and wealth of the Roman Catholic Church before the Reformation are hard to grasp today. In terms of wealth it exceeded that of the Crown, while its churchmen often played a major role in government. As patrons of architecture and the arts, the great churchmen of the later fifteenth and early sixteenth centuries were very active, often in fields beyond the strictly ecclesiastical, building themselves palaces as well as numerous lesser residences, founding colleges, maintaining great households and finally making themselves magnificent tombs. A good example is Richard Fox, successively Bishop of Exeter, Bath and Wells, Durham and Winchester, who founded Corpus Christi College, Oxford (endowing it with splendid silver), and built a palace at Norham, in Northumberland, as well as beginning a major rebuilding of the cathedral at Winchester.

The last and greatest of them all, both in terms of power and expenditure, was Cardinal Wolsey, who rose from obscurity to become the Pope's ambassador and Henry VIII's Lord Chancellor. Amassing vast sums from numerous ecclesiastical appointments and other sources, he built on a scale unmatched in his time. His projects included Hampton Court Palace (begun in 1514), York Place in London (later called Whitehall), the houses known as The More and Tyttenhanger in Hertfordshire, as well as colleges in Oxford and Ipswich. Wolsey was accused by contemporary critics of flaunting his wealth, while the scale of his building activities eventually led to them being taken into the royal domain. Only then did Henry VIII's own property begin to match that of his former Chancellor. To some extent Wolsey's building activities were justified, and in keeping with his status. The vast works at Hampton were designed to host the whole royal court (some 1,000 people) on its journeys, as well as great foreign embassies and rulers; for the highest officers of state proximity to the sovereign and helping to fulfil state business were everything.

8 The head of Bishop Fox's crozier, probably 1487–90. Silver-gilt and enamel. Corpus Christi College, Oxford.

9 Hampton Court Palace, London. Cardinal Wolsey's Hampton Court consisted of the present base court (at the bottom of this view), and the first inner court. The second inner court (greatly enlarged in 1689–95) was built by Henry VIII, who also built a new great hall (on the left).

4. Royal households and magnificence

Magnificence was the key concept of building, household and ceremony in the royal context. Henry VII built much, including Richmond Palace and chapels at Westminster and King's College, Cambridge, but his son Henry VIII built more than any other English monarch before or since. By his death he had 68 houses, amassed from dissolved monasteries and out-of-favour courtiers. While only a tiny handful of objects have survived from his court, its splendour is amply shown by the inventories. Henry's collection of tapestries was probably the biggest ever assembled, while his jewel house contained 997 items of gold, silver and jewellery at his death. In addition he had collections (then novel) of musical instruments and glass, as well as a considerable library. Much of the magnificence of the court was expressed in ephemeral events, such as masques, tournaments and other celebrations. Henry is known to have taken a close personal interest in the design and detailed arrangements of his buildings at court, especially after 1529 and Wolsey's departure from the scene, when his expenditure and building activities suddenly increased.

10

10 *The temporary palace at the Field of Cloth of Gold*, about 1545. Detail of a larger painting by an anonymous artist, recording the event of 1520.
© The Royal Collection.

5. Wolsey and Henry VIII as style innovators

We know from the accounts of contemporaries that the true test of magnificence in art and architecture in the first half of the sixteenth century was quite simply its total visual impact. It was a matter of monetary value, of complexity and curiosity of design and execution, and of sheer size. Stylistic innovation on a purely aesthetic level was unimportant and usually went unremarked. It is in this context that we should view the arrival in England of Italian Renaissance design elements and 'antique' ornament, upon which so much emphasis is placed today.

Renaissance elements had begun to arrive in England by the 1460s in the form of Italian illuminated manuscripts and, later, the decorations of printed books. Motifs from such sources passed easily to other media. The arrival of the Florentine sculptor Pietro Torrigiani, by 1511, brought Renaissance sculptural and ornamental styles as well as new techniques and uses of material. Cardinal Wolsey, who frequently went to France and the Low Countries, seems to have played a significant part in introducing Renaissance decorative motifs into the decoration of prominent permanent buildings. Most notable are the famous terracotta roundels of Roman emperors at Hampton Court, made in 1521 by Giovanni da Maiano, an Italian sculptor working in England. Significantly, they were probably economical versions of the more expensive stone portraits found on French royal buildings; even cheaper heads of Roman 'conquerors', probably made in papier mâché or plaster, were supplied by Maiano for Henry VIII's temporary 'Disguising House' for negotiations with the French in 1527. For Henry, the display of lavish and gilded classical imagery and ornament was a matter of politics, actively emulating that of his rival Francis I.

The sheer wealth of Henry VIII meant that none of his courtiers could match him in terms of expenditure, and after about 1530 the court was certainly taking the lead in taste, with its fully integrated Renaissance-style interiors on the French model. A few courtiers are known to have adopted some of these ideas in their own dwellings – for instance, Charles Brandon, the Duke of Suffolk, who had married Henry VIII's sister Mary. Both his houses, at Suffolk Place in Southwark (probably nearing completion in 1522) and Westhorpe in Suffolk (built in about 1525–35), used moulded terracotta decorations with 'antick' motifs. Another notable courtier, Sir William Sandys, Lord Chamberlain from 1526, had richly furnished king's and queen's apartments at his country house, the Vyne, Hampshire, linked by a long gallery, just like the latest arrangements at Hampton Court. The gallery was fully panelled in Gothic linenfold, but incorporating 'antique' motifs and a fine Renaissance-style coat of arms, perhaps by a court carver. In the chapel are ceramic paving tiles, imported from Antwerp, likewise decorated with 'antick' motifs. Renaissance motifs also occur in the stained glass made in Bruges for Sandys's chantry chapel in Basingstoke.

11

12

11 Decorative roundel at Hampton Court Palace, showing the Emperor Hadrian, 1521. By Giovanni da Maiano. Terracotta, formerly painted.

12 Panelling and doorway of the gallery at the Vyne, Hampshire, about 1518–26. The royal arms are flanked by the crest and shield of Sir William Sandys.

THE COURT OF HENRY VIII

Maurice Howard

The court of Henry VIII was essentially a great household that moved from place to place, as determined by seasonal activities, government business, the insatiable desire to hunt well-stocked forests and the fear of pestilence. The enormous amount of building initiated by the King meant that, by the end of his reign, more than 50 buildings could house the court. Some of these were new; some were refurbished palaces; others were houses sequestered from courtiers who had fallen from favour, or sets of lodgings adapted from parts of suppressed monasteries. Greater palaces, like Whitehall and Hampton Court, both once owned by Cardinal Wolsey, could house the whole court of several hundred people; others, like Nonsuch Palace, served as grand hunting lodges for the King, his guests and perhaps 50 servants.

The court was the place where the King's largesse, his 'magnificence', was displayed and his rivalry with European monarchs – especially Francis I of France – was played out in court ceremonial. On special occasions, such as the entertainment of the Emperor Charles V in 1522 or the Greenwich Revels of 1527, the court was the setting for great hospitality, with the building of richly decorated temporary structures in wood or canvas. Yet it is the sense of the everyday

13. Letters patent with a miniature portrait of Henry VIII, 1524. The portrait probably painted by Lucas Horenbout, also known as Hornebolte. Illuminated parchment. VAM MSL.6-1999.

maintenance of court life that comes across most strongly in the inventory of Henry's goods taken at his death in 1547.

A good many furnishings, household goods and clothes moved with the King. The court's surroundings were constantly redefined by the hanging of tapestries (more than 2,000 were recorded in 1547) in the great public rooms of each palace. The imagery of tapestry was the chief means by which the virtues of the sovereign, his military exploits and the dispensing of justice were praised through the choice of apposite classical and biblical stories. Other signs of the King's presence were his heraldry and personal badges, not only on furniture and fittings, but on the clothes worn by his servants. Alongside this, Henry increased the number of private apartments to which he could retire and it was here that more personal items were kept: the tools of daily life and administration, as well as the illuminated devotional texts and ingenious trinkets that made up the 'gift' culture of the court. The giving of presents between King and courtiers at New Year prompted the flow into court life of the latest fashions in ornament and design.

14. The Great Hall, Hampton Court Palace, London, built 1532–4 for Henry VIII.

15. Cap badge, about 1536–40. Embossed and chased gold. [diam. 4.7cm]. VAM 630-1884.

16. Stained glass showing the arms of Henry VIII and Jane Seymour, about 1536–40. Said to have come from Nonsuch Palace, Surrey. Painted and fired in England. Clear, pot-metal and flashed glass painted with brown enamel and yellow stain. [h. 45.7cm]. VAM C.454-1919.

17. Door lock, about 1539–47. Probably made by Henry Romayne(s), lockmaker to Henry VIII. Formerly on the door to the great hall of Beddington Place, Sutton, London. Gilded wrought iron. [h. 22.4cm]. VAM M.397-1921

18. Detail of a tapestry showing the story of David and Bathsheba, about 1510–15. Made in Brussels and owned by Henry VIII. Musée National de la Renaissance, Ecouen.

19. *Anne of Cleves*, 1539. By Hans Holbein the Younger. Watercolour on vellum in a contemporary turned ivory box. VAM P.153-1910.

20. Detail of a design for a royal tent, possibly for the Field of Cloth of Gold, about 1520. Watercolour on paper. The British Library.

21 Design for a gold cup for Jane Seymour, third wife of Henry VIII, 1536. By Hans Holbein the Younger. Pen, ink and wash. Ashmolean Museum.

22 Design for a fireplace for Henry VIII, about 1540. By Hans Holbein the Younger. Pen and ink and wash. The British Museum.

6. Taste and trade

The direct employment of foreign artists and craftspeople was one of the most effective ways of getting fashionable ideas from abroad. Henry VIII worked hard to entice them from rival courts, and King James V's French masons profoundly affected the style of Scottish architecture. While a number of such immigrants were French or Italian, many more came from the Low Countries, bringing Italian Renaissance forms with them. Such artists were frequently employed in a variety of fields, transferring ideas across different media, as with the Horenbout (or Hornebolte) family of illuminators from Ghent. Gerard Horenbout was also a painter and designer of tapestries, ecclesiastical vestments and stained glass. His son Luke became a pioneering miniaturist, while Wolsey's Renaissance-style seals may have been designed in the family workshop.

The German painter Hans Holbein the Younger spent two periods in England working for Henry VIII and his court. Expanding well beyond portrait painting, he designed goldsmith's work and jewellery, as well as temporary and permanent decorations and murals, and even woodcuts for the new Protestant religious books. Holbein's portraits of the German merchants of the steelyard remind us that immigrant artists' closest connections were with the more permanent foreign community whose activities as importers, or as makers, provided most of England's requirements for luxury goods, ranging from Italian silks to Flemish goldsmiths' work, right up to the middle of the seventeenth century.

7. A group of classical patrons

Henry VIII's death in 1547 marked a shift in the mechanisms of taste that was to last some 50 years, in which the lead passed from the court to the courtiers. The earliest evidence comes in the reign of his successor, the boy-king Edward VI. It was marked by a remarkable episode of stylistic innovation in architecture, namely the first serious attempt to adopt classical architecture as a system rather than a collection of disparate elements. The principal sponsor was a Protestant group around the Lord Protector himself, Edward Seymour, Duke of Somerset. Somerset was engaged in at least five building projects in the few years up to his execution in 1552, but the most important in terms of design was Somerset House in London. The pioneering French style of Somerset House can be traced in the houses of several of Somerset's associates – sometimes extending into the reign of Elizabeth I – including Sir William Sharington's Lacock in Wiltshire, Thomas Seymour's (the Protector's brother) Sudeley Castle in Gloucestershire and the Duke of Northumberland's Dudley Castle in the West Midlands. The link between them was the mason John Chapman, who went on to Longleat in Wiltshire, built by the Protector's secretary Sir John Thynne, where he developed the ideas of Somerset House. Northumberland was the employer of John Shute, whose pioneering book, *The First and Chief Groundes of Architecture*, was published in 1563. That the engraved plates in Shute's book were not directly reflected in built structures was significant only of a change in taste, for by this date printed images had become a key factor in taking design forward.

23

23 *Somerset House, The Strand, London*, built 1547–52. Detail from a plan and elevation by John Thorpe, drawn after 1611. The building was demolished in about 1777 to make way for the present Somerset House. Pen and ink. Trustees of the Sir John Soane Museum.

24

24 *Henry Howard, Earl of Surrey*, about 1546. Attributed to
William Scrots. Most of the ornamental frame with the
figures is inspired by a French Fontainebleau-school print of
the 1540s. Oil on panel. National Portrait Gallery, London.

8. Prints and taste

The invention of movable type, of printed images in woodcut, engraving and etching in books and as separate sheets had an incalculably great effect on the spread of visual ideas and aesthetic theory throughout Europe from the middle of the fifteenth century. For England, entirely dependent for its novel notions on sources from abroad, print became an especially important wellspring of new ideas after about 1560, but the presence of printed images before that date, if less directly influential, is well attested. The earliest ornament design book to be published in England, a set of moresques by Thomas Geminus, a Frenchman, was published in 1548. Significantly, it was aimed at embroiderers, many of whom were amateurs in constant need of new patterns, and at goldsmiths, who of all craftspeople had perhaps the greatest requirement to stay in the vanguard of fashion. But an English publication was exceptional, for up to the 1660s most printed visual source material came from abroad. Foreign prints lie behind the ornamental elements in portraits of the Archbishop Thomas Cranmer and Henry Howard, Earl of Surrey. Painted slightly earlier than Geminus's pattern book, they show a remarkably rapid adoption of very up-to-date motifs of the type that were used by Francis I in the palace of Fontainebleau.

The years 1560–1620 saw the peak of the influence of the foreign print in British design, matching exactly the fashion for Flemish Mannerist ornament and its associated figure subjects, notably narrative biblical stories and scenes from classical mythology. The objects affected covered a huge range, both of type and quality. All the external decoration of Wollaton Hall in Nottinghamshire, built in the 1580s and designed by Robert Smythson, was copied from a single set of images in Hans Vredeman de Vries's *Architectura*, published in 1577. Another print by him of about 1565 supplied elements in the embroidered Shrewsbury Hanging, worked by Bess of Hardwick and Mary, Queen of Scots in the 1570s. But prints were expensive. The Abbott family of Devon plasterers, and the professional embroiderer Thomas Trevelyon, had to copy prints for their own use.

The final effect was the same. Such a concentrated use of images from prints was a reflection of the need to provide ideas for a notably complex and ornament-laden style. But there would probably have been no demand for prints had high design, formerly limited to the court sphere, not been becoming less exclusive. It is significant that the end of the stream of print-derived decoration in the 1620s coincided with the return of the court to an exclusive style – that of Inigo Jones – and the development outside the court of other styles.

25

26

25 Motif for plasterwork, showing a cartouche adapted from a plate in a set of prints by Benedetto Battini, 1553. By a member of the Abbott family, probably John Abbott. Pen and ink. Devon County Record Office.

26 *A strapwork cartouche.* Plate from a set of cartouches by Benedetto Battini, published in Antwerp in 1553. Engraving on blue paper, coloured by hand. VAM 14357.9.

PRINTS AS SOURCES FOR DESIGN

Elizabeth Miller

27. *The Ill-Assorted Couple*,
about 1495. By Albrecht Dürer.
Engraving. VAM E.648-1940.

In the sixteenth and seventeenth centuries there were a number of ways in which craftspeople could secure information about new designs – from finished objects, models, drawings, or prints. Prints were the newest method of communicating design. They had originated in continental Europe in about 1400, but it was in the sixteenth century that they came increasingly to be used as sources for design in Britain.

The starting point for making a print was a flat piece of wood or a sheet of copper. Using knives and gouges on the piece of wood, and pointed tools or the action of acid on the copper, ridges were created in the wood or grooves in the copper to produce a reversed version of the desired image. These ridges or grooves were then coated or filled with ink. A blank piece of paper was pressed up against the inked wood or copper and, when the paper was peeled away, it had been printed with the image.

With each new inking, the transfer of ink from the wood or copper was repeated to produce multiple copies of the same print. Eventually the piece of wood or metal began to wear down, but not before hundreds or even thousands of copies of the print had

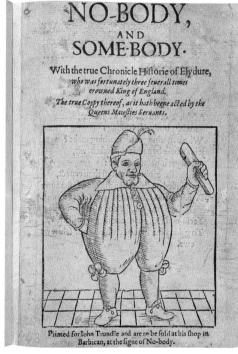

28. Misericord, Henry VII's chapel,
Westminster Abbey, London. Finished
about 1519. Adapted from Albrecht
Dürer's *The Ill-Assorted Couple*, 1495.

29. Title-page to a play,
Nobody And Somebody,
1606. Printed in London
for John Trundle.
Woodcut on paper.
VAM NAL Dyce 6967.

30. Figure of *Nobody*,
1680–5. Adapted from
the title-page to the
play *Nobody And
Somebody*. Made in
Southwark or Lambeth,
London. Tin-glazed
earthenware (delftware).
[h. 24.5cm]. VAM C.4-1982.

31. *A Ewer*, 1531. Engraved by Agostino Veneziano and published in Rome by Antonio Salamanca. Engraving. VAM 16842.

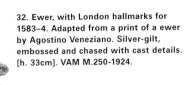

32. Ewer, with London hallmarks for 1583–4. Adapted from a print of a ewer by Agostino Veneziano. Silver-gilt, embossed and chased with cast details. [h. 33cm]. VAM M.250-1924.

33. *Abraham and the Angels*, 1585. Engraved after Maarten de Vos. From *Thesaurus Sacrarium*, published in Antwerp by Gerarde de Jode. Engraving. Fitzwilliam Museum, Cambridge.

been created. It was the existence of multiple copies of the same print that made printmaking such an effective method of spreading visual information over large distances in a short space of time, to an extent that had previously been impossible.

Prints were made of a vast variety of subjects. They were relatively inexpensive to make and buy, compared to drawings and paintings, and were light and easily transported. Some prints were produced specifically as design sources for craftspeople, but makers could – and did – draw on any print that suited their purpose. The borrowing of ideas from prints could take many forms. A two-dimensional print could be used either for the design of another flat object, as certainly happened with embroidery, or for the creation of a three-dimensional object. Sometimes the whole printed design source was reproduced in another material. Alternatively, a detail of a print could be selected for use in the design of part of a new object, or parts of two or more prints could be combined in one item.

Prints came to provide a vast pool of imagery, which makers based in Britain could trawl for the latest visual ideas from some of Europe's greatest artists and designers.

34. Detail of a cushion cover, 1640–70. The main scene adapted from a print after Maarten de Vos. The other elements taken from English prints. Non-professional embroidery over outlines drawn by a professional pattern-drawer. Linen canvas embroidered in wool and silk. [h. 55.9cm]. VAM 443-1865.

35

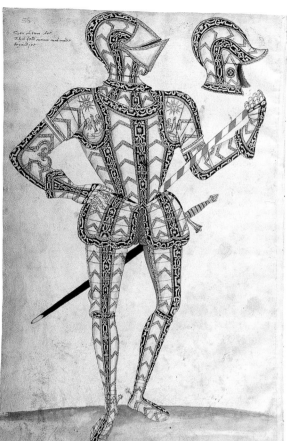

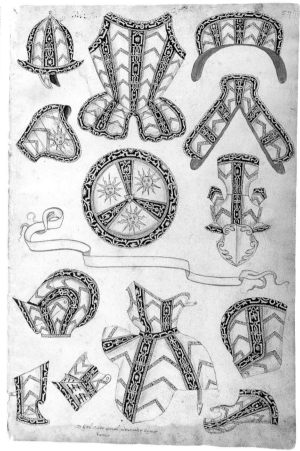

36

9. Art and politics

The period from the accession of Queen Elizabeth in 1558 to her death in 1603 was marked by an extraordinary visual culture among her leading courtiers. The Queen herself built little and, having inherited her father's vast store of goods and furnishings, was modest in her expenditure, but she was surrounded by an entire court culture in which she was increasingly celebrated as the Virgin Queen, especially from about 1580. Courtiers, as her knights, vied for her favour at annual accession-day jousts, wearing armour simultaneously real and fantastic, decorated with their emblems. The court was the nation's greatest concentration of heraldry and emblems in an age when symbolism carried all the meaning of works of art. At every level, the chivalric ideal was celebrated, with court administrators shown lying in full armour on their tombs.

According to the custom of the day, all that was the courtier's was the Queen's. This was especially so during the court's annual summer 'progress' around their country seats. While Henry VIII had also made progresses, those of Queen Elizabeth were unprecedented in their scale and the courtiers' responses to them. At Kenilworth, in 1575, for instance, Lord Robert Dudley presented her first with a vast banquet in a marquee. Later she was greeted by guns and trumpeters and by figures in fantastic costume, led by an Arthurian 'Lady of the Lake' seated on a 'movable island', reciting verses in her honour. Several days of hunting, dancing, masques and other festivities followed. The decisive move from court to courtiers is most clearly shown, however, in

35 Pendant: the Drake Jewel, the miniature dated 1588. Made in London. This jewel, given to the naval hero Sir Francis Drake, contains a portrait of Elizabeth I by Nicholas Hilliard. Courtiers frequently wore the Queen's portrait. The phoenix was the Queen's symbol. Enamelled gold with sardonyx cameo, table-cut rubies and diamonds, hung with pearls. Miniature painted in watercolour on vellum. VAM. Anonymous loan.

37

their huge 'prodigy' houses. A number of them, like Wollaton, Longleat and Burghley, survive, but even bigger structures, most notably Lord Burghley's Theobalds in Hertfordshire, have disappeared.

Far too big for the immediate domestic needs of their owners (who also had many other properties), these houses were first and foremost political statements, serving as permanent expressions of status and public office, but also, when necessary, as surrogate palaces during the Queen's progresses. The prodigy houses were remarkable exercises in taste. Many used the same Flemish Mannerist ornamental vocabulary as the applied arts of the period (and, indeed, showed a remarkable unity of style with them). But in terms of architectural design they were often novel and experimental, reflecting the need to combine the conflicting messages of chivalry and long ancestral lineage with expressions of more up-to-date (and foreign) learning, as well as the practical requirements of ceremony and status.

At Burghley, the central courtyard is surrounded by classical triumphal arches, balconies and colonnades, functioning like an arena for shows, but is topped by a huge stone pyramid supported by the family arms.

At Hardwick Hall, constructed in the 1590s, the builder and owner, Bess of Hardwick, is announced by her initials on the skyline, surmounted by a countess's coronet. Although the general impression of bays and towers recalls great courtyard houses of about 1500, huge quantities of expensive glass announce that this is a modern, outward-looking house. The increasing height of the windows clearly reveals the increasing status of the rooms within. Entrance is made through the earliest classical entrance colonnade in England, while a classical balustrade runs around the top. The interiors give us a good idea of the colourful, textile-rich rooms to which other less wealthy patrons would aspire. Bess, however, had hopes of a royal visit (which never happened) as well as a granddaughter, Arabella Stuart, with some claim to the throne. The state rooms are arranged in a sequence as in a royal palace, leading to the royal bedchamber, while their decorations carry the royal arms and an iconography related to Queen Elizabeth, subtly linked to emblems signifying Bess herself.

38 The entrance front of Hardwick Hall, Derbyshire, built 1591–7. Designed by Robert Smythson for Elizabeth Hardwick, Countess of Shrewsbury.

39 The courtyard at Burghley House, Lincolnshire, 1755. By John Haynes. Built 1555–85 for William Cecil. Pen and wash. The Burghley House Collection.

---

36 Design for armour and extra pieces, for Sir Henry Lee, 1570–5. Probably drawn by Jacob Halder, a German armourer and master workman of the Royal Armouries of Greenwich. Halder decorated the plain German cavalry armour and added pieces adapting it for infantry use and the tournament. The decoration throughout incorporates Lee's badges of the sun and falcon. Watercolour on paper. VAM D.599-1894.

37 *George Clifford, 3rd Earl of Cumberland*, about 1590. By Nicholas Hilliard. Clifford was the Queen's champion, defending her honour at the annual accession-day tilts. The combatant knights wore fancy dress: Clifford's represents the knight of Pendragon Castle – he came in riding on a horse dressed as a dragon. Watercolour on vellum laid on panel. © National Maritime Museum, London.

THE EARLY STUART COURT

Nick Humphrey

Both James I and VI and his son, Charles I, were extremely interested in art and design. They employed foreign artists and craftspeople and built up the royal collections, as well as promoting the pioneering work of Inigo Jones. Although now chiefly celebrated as an architect for his classical buildings, Jones became established at the Jacobean court as a designer – particularly of masques for Anne of Denmark. His fantastic, Italianate stage-sets, machinery and costumes for members of the court were developed in hundreds of pen-and-ink sketches. His principal building, the Whitehall Banqueting House (1619–22), was intended by James I as a formal reception chamber. The rigorous proportions and balance of Jones's modified Roman basilica interior and the Palladian façade contrasted sharply with the confusion of the Tudor Whitehall Palace. Within, Peter Paul Rubens's paintings of the life and apotheosis of James I, fixed into the compartmentalized ceiling in 1635, made explicit the building's projection of royal authority and harmony.

The promotion of tapestry was another royal endeavour. Hugely costly, tapestry production served economic, political and aesthetic ends. The Mortlake factory established in 1619 by Sir Francis Crane, using Flemish weavers, was sponsored by the Crown in emulation of Henri IV of France's Gobelin workshops. In 1623 Charles I acquired for Mortlake seven of Raphael's tapestry cartoons for the *Acts of the Apostles*, made in 1515–16.

The growing reputation of the English court encouraged foreign artists and craftspeople to come to London. The bronze founder Francesco Fanelli received a royal pension and styled himself Sculptor to the King. Orazio Gentileschi came from Paris, aged 62, and painted the allegorical ceiling canvases for the Queen's House, Henrietta Maria's riverside villa at Greenwich. Rubens's pupil Anthony Van Dyck superseded Daniel Mytens as the preferred court portraitist.

Encouraged by the example of his elder brother Henry, and by courtier-connoisseurs like the first Duke of Buckingham and the second Earl of Arundel, Charles was a knowledgeable and enthusiastic collector, though financially constrained during the period of personal rule from 1629 to 1640. In 1627 he secured through his shrewd agents a great prize for £18,000, the collections of the Duke of Mantua, bringing to London more of the Venetian paintings he loved, as well as outstanding contemporary works, important antique sculpture and Andrea Mantegna's *Triumphs of Caesar*. The last were retained by Cromwell when most of the royal art collections were sold in 1649.

40. The interior of the Banqueting House at Whitehall, London, 1619–22. Designed by Inigo Jones.

41. *Charles I, Queen Henrietta Maria, Prince Charles and Princess Mary,* 1632. By Sir Anthony Van Dyck. Oil on canvas. © The Royal Collection.

42. Tapestry, *The Miraculous Draught of Fishes from the Acts of the Apostles,* 1637–8. The central scene designed by Raphael. Woven at the Mortlake tapestry factory, London. Made for Philip Herbert, Earl of Pembroke. VAM Loan: Buccleuch. I.

43. *Saint George and the Dragon,* about 1640. By Francesco Fanelli. Cast bronze. [h. 19.1cm]. VAM A.5-1953.

44. Two costume designs for the King and Queen, for the masque, from *Salmacida Spolia,* written by Sir William D'Avenant, 1640. By Inigo Jones. Pen and brown ink, one over grey wash. Devonshire Collection, Chatsworth.

10. A new court

The triumphal entry of James I and VI into London in 1604 was a public celebration unmatched since the days of Henry VIII. Seven great arches were the stages for orations and songs composed by celebrated dramatists. Clothed in Flemish Mannerist ornament (and based on those used for the entry into Antwerp of Archduke Albert and the Infanta Isabella in 1599), the arches were nevertheless designed to modular proportions answering the musical harmonies. This great event marked the return of the court to the centre of visual culture. From the start, more money was spent: the pageantry of the entry alone cost more than was expended on all such events during the reign of Elizabeth I, while James immediately set about replacing with modern plate the 14,000 troy ounces (435 kilograms) of old silver that he had given away at the accession. The size of the royal family was a key factor, with separate palaces being fitted out for the King, Queen and Henry, Prince of Wales.

James I and VI's international outlook, coinciding with a period of peace in Europe, finally opened up British visual culture to the Renaissance tradition in architecture and the visual arts. This process was pursued, in different ways, by a number of individuals at court, including James and Queen Anne, the connoisseur and collector Earl of Arundel and the court architect Inigo Jones. It was continued by Charles I and his queen, Henrietta Maria. Jones, who worked for all these patrons, was a key figure. As well as being a brilliant and

46

45

original architect, he was a court designer in the European tradition, able to turn his hand to most designing tasks; starting with masque designs, he moved on to buildings and then interiors. His great aim, as expressed in 1606 by his friend the antiquarian Edmund Bolton, was that 'all that is praiseworthy in the elegant arts of the ancients, may some day insinuate themselves across the Alps into our England'. This aim was shown as much in his masque designs, which introduced numerous ideas from Italy and France, as in his buildings, which for the first time in England showed a proper understanding of the nature of classical architecture.

45 *Inigo Jones*, 1655. By Wenceslaus Hollar after a drawing of 1640 by Sir Anthony Van Dyck. Engraving. VAM Circ.116-1967.

46 *The Pegme of the Dutchmen*, a triumphal arch made for the procession of James I and VI through the City of London in March 1604. Engraved by William Kip and published by Stephen Harrison as part of the set, *Arch's of Triumph*, 1604. Engraving. VAM 14008.

11. Art at court

The Stuart court was the first in Britain to patronize and collect painting and sculpture for their own sake, rather than for their subjects. Charles I, especially, raced to make up for artistic lost ground by seeking to employ the most famous artists from abroad. For a few years, until they were dispersed under the Commonwealth, the art collections of the British court exceeded in quality those of most foreign competitors. The new pastime of collecting Italian and other modern painting and sculpture was matched by the habit (also of Italian origin) of assembling collections of classical sculpture and other antiquities, rarities and 'objects of virtue'.

Most active in this field was the second Earl of Arundel, one of the key figures in the intended revival in the arts and learning. The Earl's collections, built up from 1612, included inlaid Italian furniture, a famous collection of paintings by Holbein, the celebrated 'Arundel marbles' and more than 200 albums of Italian Renaissance drawings. The trips to the continent that formed a vital part of Arundel's artistic education were pioneering examples of the Grand Tour, an experience that was to become key in forming the tastes of the ruling classes. In 1613 Arundel took with him Inigo Jones, to whom this Italian trip was crucial. He met Vincenzo Scamozzi, the stylistic disciple of Andrea Palladio, acquired Palladio drawings and studied his buildings systematically at first hand, acquiring a profound critical knowledge of classical architecture.

In 1615 Jones took up the post of Surveyor of the King's Works, in charge of all royal building activity. He was an architect of recognizably modern type, a single controlling mind able to work out a whole building on paper and see it built as it was drawn. This was something completely new in Britain – not because of Jones's brilliance (undoubted though it was), but because before the advent of the symmetrical certainties and systems of classicism, with its logically related plans, elevations and sections, it was simply not possible to be certain of built outcomes. This new approach, which did not reach all building until about 1700, had a profound effect on the origination and transmission of design ideas, enabling architects to be certain of their intended results, and allowing architectural ideas to travel without distortion via books and prints.

47 *Thomas Howard, 2nd (Howard) Earl of Arundel and Surrey*, about 1618. By Daniel Mytens. The Earl points to the sculpture gallery on the first floor of Arundel House, London. Some of the statues had been brought back from Italy in 1614. Oil on canvas. National Portrait Gallery, London.

The sophisticated clarity, proportion and appropriate grandeur of Jones's few buildings were at first appreciated only by a tiny cultured élite, but their effect was like a time-bomb. The Banqueting House (1619–22) was the prototype for palace-like government buildings from the 1660s onwards. The Queen's House at Greenwich (1616–35) and the Prince's Lodging at Newmarket (1619–21) became the touchstones of the neo-Palladian revival a hundred years later. But it was in urban building that Jones's ideas were to have the greatest immediate impact. The arcaded scheme at Covent Garden (1631–7), put up by the Earl of Bedford, was one of the origins of the London square and quickly established the idea of the classical terraced building. Details of Jonesian origin, such as the iron balcony or 'pergula' (which, according to the antiquary John Bagford, 'country folks were much wont to gaze upon'), became part of the builder's baroque composite style now known as 'artisan Mannerism'.

In the broadest sense, a classical form of building, however varied in detail, had become the norm by about 1660. By this stage, too, as James Cleland wrote as early as 1607 in *The institution of a young noble man*, 'the principles of architecture . . . [are] also necessary for a gentleman to be known', as was a knowledge of painting and sculpture. This educational process was assisted by a steadily increasing number of books in English about architecture and the visual arts from about 1600, and especially after 1660. Up to 1715 they were, significantly, nearly all translations of French or Italian texts. One of the few exceptions was *Elements of Architecture* of 1624 by Sir Henry Wotton, the

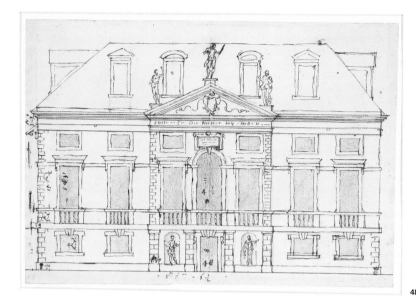

48

ambassador in Venice. Experience abroad was seen as essential for designing buildings, especially after 1660, when Sir Roger Pratt advised that 'if you be not able to handsomely contrive it [a suitable design] yourself', then it was necessary to get at least a sketch 'from some ingenious gentleman who has seen much of that kind abroad', as well as to have read the right books. The only buildings considered worth inspecting in England were the Banqueting House and Inigo Jones's colonnade at St Paul's Cathedral.

49

48 *Design for the Prince's Lodging, Newmarket Palace, Suffolk*, 1619. By Inigo Jones. Pen, ink and wash. RIBA Library Drawings Collection.

49 *Covent Garden on a Market Day*, about 1756–8. By Samuel Scott. Inigo Jones designed the arcaded buildings on the right (1631–7) and the church of St Paul on the left (1631–3). The Museum of London.

12. Fashion from abroad: the court of Charles II

Pratt was one of many who had been forced abroad by the political events of the 1640s and 1650s. On his return he became an influential gentleman architect (see Chapter 2), notably through his house for the Earl of Clarendon in Piccadilly.

The shift in taste that occurred after the King's return in 1660 is clearly shown in two reactions to Clarendon House. Firstly, to John Evelyn, Pratt's friend and fellow continental traveller, it was simply 'the best contriv'd, most useful, most graceful, and magnificent house in England. I except not Audley-end [a house he had admired in 1654]; which though larger, and full of gaudy & barbarous ornaments, does not gratify judicious spectators'. Samuel Pepys, too, changed his opinion of Audley End, praising the huge Jacobean house in 1660, but, after visiting Clarendon House in 1667, finding it old-fashioned after the 'nobleness' and 'furniture and pictures' of the London house: 'the ceilings are not so good as I took them to be, being nothing so well wrought as my Lord Chancellor's are; and though the figure of the house without be extraordinary good, yet the staircase is exceeding poor'.

Pepys's concentration on the interiors of both buildings, and his continuing approval of the *exterior* of Audley End, reminds us that one of the principal effects of Charles II's exile and triumphant return was the introduction of new forms of interior decoration and ornament. These were created in emulation of foreign courts, and especially that of France. The survival of great courtier houses like Chatsworth and Petworth and the destruction or alteration of all Charles II's significant palace projects, including Wren's royal palace at Winchester and most of the great baroque interiors of the 1670s at Windsor Castle, have obscured the pioneering nature of court building and decoration. Only the reduced echoes still seen at Windsor and at the Scottish Palace of Holyroodhouse serve to remind us of the achievements in plaster and paint that were so influential.

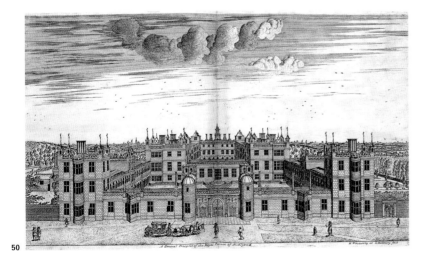

50 Audley End, Essex, built 1603–14. Engraved by Henry Winstanley, about 1676. Engraving. VAM E.343-1902.

51 Clarendon House, Piccadilly, London, built about 1670. By John Dunstall. Clarendon House, designed by Sir Roger Pratt, was built in 1664–7 and demolished in 1683. Etching. VAM E.426-1898.

52 The Great Hall at Audley End, Essex, built 1603–14.

53

55

54

The accessibility of Charles II's court, in contrast to that of Charles I, not only opened it up to censure on moral grounds, but exposed private royal tastes to a greater number of people. Evelyn was shocked at the luxury displayed therein, although he approved of appropriate grandeur on the exteriors of royal buildings. Writing in 1683 about the dressing room of the King's mistress, the Duchess of Portsmouth, he commented:

> ... what ingag'd my curiosity, was the rich & splendid furniture of this woman's apartment, now once or twice puld down and rebuilt, to satisfie her prodigal and expensive pleasures . . . : Here I saw the new fabrique of *French Tapissry*, for design, tendernesse of worke, & incomparable imitation of the best paintings; beyond anything, I had ever beheld ...Then for *Japon Cabinets*, *Skreenes*, *Pendule* Clocks, Huge *Vasas* of wrought plate, *Tables*, *Stands*, *Chimny furniture*, *Sconces*, branches, *Braseras* &c they were all of massive silver and without number, besides of his Majesties best paintings ...

But Evelyn was in the minority, for by this stage the royal lead was eagerly being followed by courtiers, who were busily ordering state beds and creating apartments *en enfilade*. At Ham House, which, Evelyn said, was 'furnished like a great Prince's', the Duke of Lauderdale created these features in rooms

53 The king's ante-chamber, the Palace of Holyroodhouse, Edinburgh. Holyroodhouse was enlarged and remodelled in 1671–9 to the designs of Sir William Bruce. The plasterwork was by John Houlbert and George Dunsterfield.

54 The Queen's closet, Ham House, London, about 1675.

built in the 1670s. Some 25 great state beds survive from this period up to about 1700. In the 1680s courtiers, who had left off large building projects since the early years of the century, started to put up country houses on a palatial scale. The earliest, the Earl of Devonshire at Chatsworth, employed all the carvers, painters, smiths and other craftspeople being used on the royal works, although other noblemen did not stint on importing their own craftspeople and painters from France, as the Duke of Montagu did for Montagu House in the early 1690s. However, royal influence was not simply a matter of art and design, but of complete court etiquette. The King played a key role in introducing as court dress the wearing of the Persian vest in deliberate opposition to French fashion, during hostilities with France in 1666, in order that, according to Lord Halifax, 'we might look like a more distinct people'.

Foreign artists and craftspeople became especially important in the process of creating the Franco-Dutch court style after 1660.

Sometimes opposition from the London trade guilds was overcome by their employment in the royal office of the Great Wardrobe, which was outside guild control. Perhaps significantly (in view of Evelyn's comments), the Flemish painter Sir Peter Lely was largely employed to paint private images of Charles II's mistresses, while the English painter John Michael Wright did the King's state portraits. Antonio Verrio (brought to England by the Duke of Montagu in 1672) introduced the art of *trompe l'oeil* baroque mural painting.

Foreign craftspeople became especially evident in the 1680s, when the accession of William and Mary made Britain a particularly suitable destination for several thousand Huguenots fleeing France, following the revocation of the Edict of Nantes in 1685, which took away their protection. The high technical expertise of Huguenot goldsmiths, gunmakers, clockmakers, silk weavers, ironsmiths and others was at least as important as

---

55 *The Duchess of Portsmouth*, about 1679. By Sir Peter Lely. Oil on canvas. Atkinson Art Gallery, Southport.

56 The chapel, Chatsworth House, Derbyshire, built 1688–93. Painting by Louis Laguerre, Ricard and Antonio Verrio. Carving by Caius Gabriel Cibber, Samuel Watson and Grinling Gibbons.

57 *Charles II*, 1671. By John Michael Wright. Oil on canvas. © The Royal Collection.

THE MELVILLE BED

Tessa Murdoch

The accession of William and Mary in 1689 inspired a new confidence in the monarchy. A spate of rebuilding and redecoration of the royal palaces was imitated by leading courtiers and officers of state. This resulted in a crop of grand British houses in the baroque style.

In 1689 George Melville was appointed Secretary of State for Scotland and in 1690 William III made him an earl. From 1691 Melville held other lesser offices of state with lucrative salaries. In 1697 he commissioned a palatial residence, Melville House, Fife, from the leading Scottish architect James Smith.

The highlight of the State Apartment on the first floor was the State Bedroom, with its magnificent bed hung with crimson Genoa velvet and lined with ivory Chinese damask. Like the entrance doorway and the carved overmantels, the State Bed was decorated with symbols of Melville's authority – earl's coronets – and personalized with ciphers of his initials and those of his wife, Catherine. The marriage was of dynastic importance; she was the daughter of Alexander, first Earl of Leven, and brought that title into the Melville family.

The bed was inspired by the work of Daniel Marot, the French-trained designer to William and Mary, whose work in interiors and garden layouts Lord Melville would have seen during his exile in Holland in the 1680s. Marot's designs, published from 1687, provided a rich source for contemporary craftspeople. The bed

58. *George, 1st Earl of Melville*, **1691. By Sir John Baptiste de Medina. Oil on canvas. Scottish National Portrait Gallery.**

is attributed to the French émigré upholsterer Francis Lapiere, who worked in Pall Mall, St James's, London.

As the dominant piece of furniture in the palatial, but often rarely used apartments of state that became a feature of noble houses in the late seventeenth century, beds of this kind were not intended for regular sleeping. Rather they symbolized their owner's wealth, noble rank and exalted connections. On the few occasions they were used, it was by illustrious visitors, usually royalty. Then they became a majestic theatrical setting where the visitor received privileged guests according to strict rules of precedence. Only the prodigiously wealthy could afford to spend so much on a little-used symbol of their eminent status.

59. Headboard of the State Bed from Melville House.

60. *Catherine, 1st Countess of Melville*, **1691. By Sir John Baptiste de Medina. Oil on canvas. In a private Scottish collection.**

61. The State Bed from
Melville House, Fife, about
1700. Probably upholstered
by Francis Lapiere and
assembled in London. Bed
stock of oak, tester of pine,
hangings of crimson Italian
velvet with ivory Chinese silk
linings, embroidered with
crimson braid and fringe.
[h. 462.3cm].
VAM W.35-1949.

62

13. Classicism established

The years after 1660 fulfilled the aspirations of Charles I and Inigo Jones to create a new national architecture expressed in the classical style. This was principally the achievement of Sir Christopher Wren. We should not be surprised, given the period's importance as a cradle of experimental science, that Wren began as a distinguished scientist, Professor of Astronomy and founder of the Royal Society, for contemporaries like Evelyn believed that architecture was 'the flower and crown as it were of all the sciences mathematical'. Indeed, it was Wren's work as a scientist that first attracted the King's attention in 1660, leading to his eventual appointment as Surveyor General of the King's Works in 1668. Wren was a brilliant empirical designer, capable of working in a number of different classical styles drawn from a wide range of sources. Most significantly, he operated almost entirely in the public arena. Some of his designs, such as most of his palace schemes, were either never built or were truncated in their execution, but his built public work, and especially St Paul's Cathedral and the City churches after the Fire of London, affected church building right into the nineteenth century and secular building up to the 1720s, establishing a consistent public architecture in Britain for the first time.

This process went hand-in-hand with the development of the King's Office of Works, which became, in effect, a training school for architects, builders and other craftspeople. The consequences were profound. In the long term it represented the first step towards the creation of a real architectural profession; more immediately it was a mechanism for the spread of design ideas through the subsequent work of the participating masons and other master craftspeople, both for exteriors and interiors. While the craftspeople and builders followed Wren's style, leading to the creation of a national school, his assistants and distinguished colleagues, like Nicholas Hawksmoor and Sir John Vanbrugh, went their own way stylistically, creating a new and dramatic baroque style.

the fashions they brought, allowing them to keep up with changing French tastes through networks of their compatriots on the continent. The immigrants also added to the growing quantity of ornament prints published in England after 1660. Their mixed nature, a combination of reissues of old sets and copies of new ones from abroad, is a clear indication of a great demand for guidance in the new styles.

An Act of God can also be said to have had a profound and long-term effect on architecture and planning. A few days after most of the City had been burned down in the Great Fire of 1666, Wren presented the King with a scheme to rebuild London on a regular plan. This came to nothing, but in the same year Wren, Pratt and the royal architect Hugh May were among the commissioners considering the rebuilding and helped to draft the Rebuilding Act of 1667. This was the first of many statutes that regulated building in the City of London (and, after 1774, beyond it as well), marking the true end of haphazard medieval building and

63

---

62 Dish and ewer, with London hallmarks for 1705–6. Made and engraved by Philip Rollos and supplied by John Charleton, Master of the Jewel Office, as ambassadorial plate for Thomas Wentworth, Baron Raby and third Earl of Strafford, as Ambassador Extraordinary to the King of Prussia. Silver-gilt, engraved and cast with applied ornament. VAM M.23-1963.

63 *Designs for an écuelle and lid*, 1694. By C. de Moelder. Plate from the set *Proper Ornaments to be Engrav'd on Plate*. The ecuelle (porringer) was introduced into Britain by Huguenot craftspeople. Engraving and stipple engraving. VAM E.386-1926.

design practices, which had been the subject of fitful regulation for some 60 years. Among other things, the Act established four sorts of flat-fronted house, related in height to the width of the street and with a fixed number of floors at fixed distances. The purpose of regulation was not simply to allow in light and air (and prevent fire) but to control appropriate occupation, from the houses of the first, two-storey sort in 'by-streets and lanes' to the 'Citizens of Extraordinary quality' in the third sort, 'fronting high and principal streets'. A sumptuary law by another name, it was created at a time when other forms of consumption were beginning to move away from such controls, as taste moved into the Georgian period. But that is another story.

64 St Paul's Cathedral. London, built 1675–1710. Designed by Sir Christopher Wren.

65 *Sir Christopher Wren*, 1711. By Sir Godfrey Kneller. Oil on canvas. National Portrait Gallery, London.

66 No. 10, Neville's Court, London, built about 1680–1700. A house of the second sort, as established by the Rebuilding Act of 1667.

CHAPTER 4

Fashionable living

MAURICE HOWARD

1. The impact of change

In the modern world we have got used to the idea that our lives are subject to change. We may mix and match the fashions of a few years ago with those of the present, but we all accept that the houses we live in, the goods amassed there and the clothes that we wear will look fundamentally different at one end of our lives from the other.

In the sixteenth and seventeenth centuries people in Britain had to come to terms with the impact of change in new and challenging ways. The Reformation radically changed fundamentals of belief and systems of authority within the Church and redistributed between one-quarter and one-third of the country's land. The great inflation of about 1550 challenged previous certainties about economic stability. The political upheavals of the seventeenth century saw a king executed and another forced into exile, with permanent impact on the power of the monarchy. All these moves suggested that political, economic and social structures were impermanent and encouraged a new, sober judgement on change in matters of everyday life.

1 Paycocke's House, Great Coggeshall, Essex, built about 1500 for Thomas Paycocke, chief clothier of the town.

2 *Sir Thomas More and his family*, 1527–8. By Hans Holbein the Younger. Preparatory drawing for a lost life-size painting. This is one of very few contemporary depictions of an early 16th-century English domestic interior. Pen and ink. Öffentliche Kunstsammlung, Basel.

In his *Description of England*, first published in 1577, the Essex clergyman William Harrison perceived change in terms of economic prosperity expanding down through the social classes; barons, the lowest rank of nobility, could now, he argued, afford new houses of a scale formerly reserved for great princes, and 'inferior artificers and many farmers' have 'learned also to garnish their cupboards with plate, their joint beds with tapestry and silk hangings, and their tables with carpets and fine napery, whereby the wealth of our country . . . doth infinitely appear'. By the time Daniel Defoe compiled *A Tour through the Whole Island of Great Britain* in the 1720s, the change that Harrison had described was being explained in terms of great cycles of the rise and fall of cities, important families, harbours and manufactures, but his comments were also infused with a sense of the new 'Empire' of Great Britain as a net exporter of ideas and products, in command of change and thus of its destiny.

When examining the houses and disposable goods that made up the day-to-day of people's lives it is important to stress two things, firstly about quantity and availability, and secondly about the dominant market. One of the ways of gauging the greater availability of objects in the home is to judge aspects of use, and it does appear that while a great many items in the house of about 1500 might be new (or certainly renewable, according to the dictates of fashion), the vast majority were objects that were in daily use; few things were superfluous or decorative. By 1700 many more objects were kept for the sake of decoration and for their value as collectable items; indeed, among the most wealthy the growth of collecting, and the discrimination that went with that development of taste, forms a key feature of the story of the arts in the seventeenth century.

In the early seventeenth century a handful of leading collectors gathered antique sculpture and other antiquities, alongside paintings and drawings recognized as great achievements of the Italian and Flemish schools of artists. By 1700 collecting had expanded to include contemporary work and examples from a range of the decorative arts. The first collections of contemporary delftware were being assembled, led by the example of Queen Mary II, celebrating the finest and rarest manufactures that were on offer. Netherlandish delftware had already been copied by English factories at Lambeth and Bristol.

William Harrison used the evidence of houses as an indicator of improved living conditions. He especially noted the greater adoption of permanent materials, the importance of larger living spaces and the rethinking of parts of the house in relation to each other: 'The ancient manors and houses of our gentlemen are yet, and for the most part, of strong timber . . . Howbeit, such as be lately builded are commonly either of brick or hard stone or both, their rooms large and comely, and houses of office [i.e. kitchens, rooms for storage, stables] further distant from their lodgings.' He was writing, however, only at the beginning of a great upturn in building activity. The period from about 1570 has often been described as an age of the 'Great Rebuilding' of the country's domestic housing, which continued until the early eighteenth century, interrupted to some extent by the disruption of the civil war of 1640–60.

3 *A Magnificent Mansion lately standing in Crutched Friars*, 1792. By J. T. Smith. Showing the courtyard of an elaborate London house of about 1600. Engraving. Corporation of London.

3

2. House planning

The initial phase of this regeneration witnessed great changes in the interior planning of houses, which reflected greater prosperity for some, new ideas about privacy and convenience and, in the grandest houses, new concepts of demonstrating wealth and splendour for entertaining and impressing one's peer group. Various styles of exterior architecture were successively employed – sometimes to express, at other times to disguise, changes within. After about 1660, however, a second phase of great rebuilding saw the emergence of a new conformity of style in the exterior of houses in both town and country. This evolved from the architectural logic of the classical style, with its symmetry and proportion, its clear sense of how to express the more and less important parts of a building through a standard vocabulary of ornament. This overlay of classicism proved the ultimate means of harmonizing external order with the new internal arrangements of houses.

In the largest houses, built for the nobility and the wealthiest of gentry landowners, the increase in the number of room spaces marked a greater concern for privacy, for separating masters and servants and thereby abandoning the provision of the communal living spaces that had marked great houses at an earlier period. The hall, once a communal living and often sleeping space, had by this time become more of a vestibule, a circulation or crossing point between the various rooms of the house. There was also a sense of other rooms now having specialist functions.

In the first half of the sixteenth century great houses were often built around courtyards, essentially planned as separate ranges with different roles in servicing the house. There was no sense of external symmetry or order, save that afforded by the material employed: brick largely in the south and east of England, stone in the West Country and in Scotland. The building was understood externally by a kind of applied sign language indicating the various parts: coats of arms over gateways, bay windows to important rooms and tower structures. These last often had an added floor to indicate the owner's privacy and as a place for the security of goods. The concern for heraldry to denote both the hierarchy of the house and the importance of its owner found its way also, within the house, into stained glass, wall hangings and fittings such as tiles.

4 The south front of Belton House, Lincolnshire, built 1685–6 for Sir John Brownlow.

5 Armorial floor tile, 1500–21. Made in the Worcester area for Edward Stafford, Duke of Buckingham, for use at Thornbury Castle, Gloucestershire. Red earthenware, stamped and filled with white clay slip. VAM 1098-1892.

6 Stained-glass panel from Beaupré Hall, Cambridgeshire, about 1570. It shows the arms of the 16th-century owner's great-grandfather, stressing his ancestry. Clear, flashed and pot-metal glass painted with brown enamel and yellow stain. VAM C.60-1946.

GREAT HOUSE LAYOUTS

Sara Pennell

The diplomat and scholar Henry Wotton declared in 1624 that, to the English gentleman, the 'proper mansion house' was 'the theatre of his hospitality, the seat of self-fruition,...the noblest of his son's inheritance, a kind of private princedom...an epitome of the whole world'. The great house of the sixteenth and seventeenth centuries was indeed the key visible symbol articulating not only architectural tastes, but also the power and status, of its inhabitants.

Compton Wynyates was completed in the 1520s by Henry VIII's courtier, Sir William Compton. It retained central features of late-medieval domestic organization: a great hall with, at one end, service rooms separated off by a screens passage and, at the other, a parlour with a chamber above it. In adopting a traditional courtyard arrangement for his house, Compton stressed the pre-eminence of protecting the community that lived within, rather than pursuing external display through Renaissance-inspired iconographic schemes or symmetry.

7. Compton Wynyates, Warwickshire, completed in the 1520s.

9. The Great Hall, Compton Wynyates, looking towards the screens passage and service rooms. Compton Wynyates, Warwickshire.

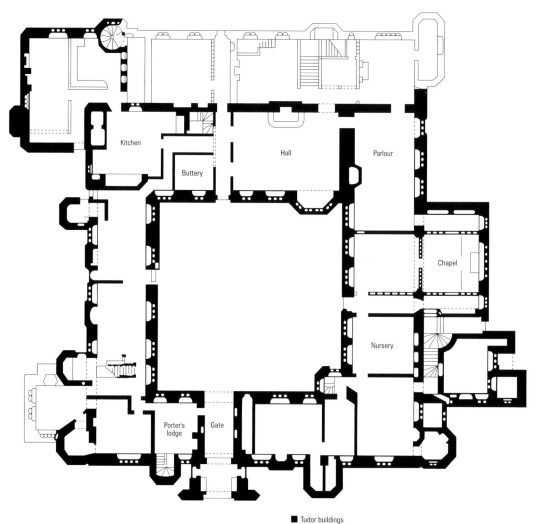

8. Conjectural plan of the ground floor of Compton Wynyates, Warwickshire, about 1520.

Kitchen

Buttery

Hall

Parlour

Chapel

Nursery

Porter's lodge

Gate

■ Tudor buildings
□ Additions after 1600

By the end of the sixteenth century symmetry and statements of splendour were in the ascendant. Key medieval features, not least the great hall and chapel, remained at the heart of many structures, but other spaces and the decoration of external and internal surfaces expressed the complex collision of Renaissance precepts with Elizabethan enthusiasm for spectacle. Aston Hall (begun about 1618), symmetrical on all four façades, with lofty gables and copious glazing, realized this complexity internally, too. Its 39-metre long gallery, with its intricate plaster ceiling and arcaded panelling, linked the formal and less formal wings of the house. Yet, as a place of both recreation and display, it belonged to neither category.

Aston had a suite of fine rooms for honoured guests, but the fullest realization of the State Apartment to articulate social hierarchy came later in the seventeenth century. Sequences of palatial rooms,

10. The Long Gallery, Aston Hall, Birmingham.

11. The east front of Aston Hall, Birmingham, 1618–35. Designed by John Thorpe for Sir Thomas Holte.

designed to 'filter' access to the monarch by guests and courtiers according to their status, were a continental innovation. In England such sequences were most fully achieved at royal palaces like Hampton Court, but the landed élite were also keen to incorporate 'apartments of state' into their seats, in expectation of a royal visit. Between 1698 and 1704 William Blathwayt, a successful government official under William III, built just such an enfilade of rooms at Dyrham Park. Filled with costly furnishings like the great State Bed, they often lay unused, 'more for State than use except upon Extraordinary occasion', as Blathwayt's cousin John Povey noted. Neither bed nor apartments was ever used for a royal visit in Blathwayt's lifetime.

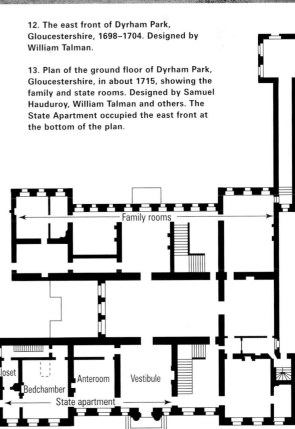

12. The east front of Dyrham Park, Gloucestershire, 1698–1704. Designed by William Talman.

13. Plan of the ground floor of Dyrham Park, Gloucestershire, in about 1715, showing the family and state rooms. Designed by Samuel Hauduroy, William Talman and others. The State Apartment occupied the east front at the bottom of the plan.

Family rooms

Closet
Bedchamber
Anteroom
Vestibule
State apartment

14. Enfilade through the rooms at Dyrham Park, built about 1698–1704, terminating in a *trompe l'oeil* painting. Painting by Samuel Hoogstraten, 1662. The National Trust.

The later sixteenth century saw grand houses with just as large a floor area, but now integrated into compact blocks, with courtyards increasingly abandoned and a clear articulation of separate floor levels. The demarcation of functions of the house by floor level eventually prompted the regular application of classical orders to the exterior. It was members of the gentry and of the wealthy urban middling class who led the way in the demand for compact houses in both town and country. Compactness and consistency of floor levels led in turn, both externally and internally, to a new concept of design. Rooms that once would have been arranged with purely functional considerations in mind, leading off each other where practical needs determined and with larger or smaller windows according to the room's importance, were now arranged in *enfilade*, with doors from one room to another aligned to create a regular vista. This regularity meant that conventions of decoration and furnishing could become more standardized and the furnishings of each particular space more *en suite* with each other. The earlier loose association of internal spaces had by 1700 become organized into sets of rooms.

It was in Scotland that the modern form of 'hall' was first given a correct, descriptive name, for it there became known as the 'lobby', indicating its function as vestibule. In Scotland the word 'hall' usually meant a grand reception room, more akin to the space in England known as a 'great chamber'. This room was often reserved in great houses for special occasions and would, in the grandest houses, serve as the place of reception for visitors of high rank, perhaps for dining in at particular times of year and even as a

15

16

15 The winter parlour, Canons Ashby, Northamptonshire, with painted decoration of the 1590s.

16 The long gallery, Haddon Hall, Derbyshire, built about 1600. This gallery was built as an extension to an earlier courtyard house, forming one side of a second court and overlooking the gardens.

place for the lying-in-state of the dead body of a high-ranking owner. The great chamber was on the upper floor of the house, while a downstairs room retained the name 'parlour' well into the seventeenth century and was the family room of common daily life. 'Drawing room' generally supplanted the term 'great chamber' in the seventeenth century, though a number of drawing rooms proliferated in larger houses. Sometimes the word 'saloon' – derived from the French *salon* and denoting the predominance of French fashions in interior furnishing – was used for the chief reception room.

Throughout the sixteenth century and in many parts of the country even beyond 1600, particularly in rural areas or less fashionable country houses, inventories of household possessions tell us that many rooms in the house still contained beds. Some great houses had a 'best' bedchamber, indicating a room probably reserved for visitors, but a significant development of the seventeenth century was the emergence of a 'state' bedchamber: part of a sequence of rooms, for which an especially grand bed would be commissioned. The bedchamber would be preceded by at least one room for private reception by an important visitor, and followed by a small, inner room closer to the bedroom – the whole set of rooms making up an 'apartment', a term derived from the French, with whom the idea began. In the largest houses two suites of such rooms were provided for the honoured visitor and for his wife, the plan of these matching rooms echoing each other across the main floor of the house. One remarkable feature attending this development, however, was the disappearance of regular provision, in new houses after about 1550, for sanitation. Late medieval and early Tudor houses usually had garderobe offshoots acting as lavatories wherever they were needed, disgorging into moats or into a pit that was periodically emptied. The increase of formality in architecture meant that these 'necessaries' as outshoots from the building were more difficult to place and disguise (though sometimes the sides of huge fireplace projections were used). Greater privacy may have meant that inner closets could now provide the place for a personal close stool, attended to by the servant who slept nearby.

The greater formality of planning the important rooms of a house was tied to a greater expectation of daily ceremonial in the household and, on the occasion of important visits, places that could be shown as a sign of family status. One especially notable feature of the greater country houses of these two centuries (and even of larger town houses where this proved convenient) was the provision of a long gallery. This originated as a means of access into the gardens, along the sides of courtyards linking parts of the building to one another or running alongside a sequence of rooms to provide a communal passage of communication. By the Elizabethan and Jacobean period long galleries were on a grand scale, in the largest houses being built high in the house underneath the roof to overlook parkland and forest, and usually containing some of the finest family possessions, including portraits.

3. Wall and ceiling decoration

The fitting out of a house began from practical concerns, but increasingly offered a choice of materials as the period progressed. Wall coverings were important for the exclusion of draughts. Panelling, in oak and usually painted throughout this period, developed from a piecemeal art of small panels attached to battens, the panels often being decorated with a pattern of folded cloth, later called 'linenfold'. From the later sixteenth century inlaid woods were more often employed and the arrangement of panelling became grander, devised architecturally with dado and cornice, perhaps also with pilasters in the main field, thus echoing the order of exterior architecture, especially for large rooms such as main drawing rooms (or saloons) and long galleries. In this new architectural scheme the fireplace became a focal point, with the generally lower fireplaces of early Tudor times now giving way to larger, grander fire openings with overmantels, carrying heraldry or allegorical subjects, in carved wood or alabaster.

As an alternative to panelling, textile hangings might cover a wall. The wealth of hangings was certainly the most distinctive feature of a room, especially when associated with textiles on accompanying furniture, and often gave the name to a particular room in the house to distinguish it from others.

17

17 Detail of a panelled room known as the 'Haynes Grange Room', created about 1585–1620, perhaps for Chicksands Priory, Bedfordshire. The interior architecture created here partly followed woodcuts for Sebastiano Serlio's third book on architecture (first published 1540), in which he described the interior of the Pantheon in Rome. This photograph shows the panelling as re-erected at the Victoria and Albert Museum in 1929. VAM W.1-1929.

18

19

18 Tapestry showing the arms of the Earl of Leicester, about 1585. Probably made at one of the Sheldon tapestry workshops in Warwickshire or Worcestershire, for Leicester House, near the Thames, the London house of Robert Dudley, Earl of Leicester. Tapestry woven in wool and silk. [h. 290cm]. VAM T.320-1977.

19 Tapestry showing the Judgement of Paris, about 1595. Made at one of the Sheldon tapestry workshops in Warwickshire or Worcestershire, for Chastleton House, Oxfordshire. Tapestry woven in wool and silk. [h. 321cm]. VAM T.310-1920.

At the highest end of the market, tapestry, imported from Flanders or subsequently supplied by the Mortlake tapestry factory founded in the reign of James I and VI, carried grand themes, still sometimes biblical (though with a narrower choice of subjects and stories, after the Reformation discouraged the depiction of certain mystical Christian themes) or from classical literature or ancient history. Dense landscapes set in the heart of woodland evoked the necessary pastime of hunting, which was so integral to life on the country estate. Cheaper stained and painted cloths hung in less important rooms, or throughout the main living spaces in less important houses. Style changed much less in these over two centuries, so that the few surviving fragments of this material are often difficult to date. There was a vogue in the seventeenth century for hangings of gilded or painted leather, usually imported from the Low Countries. However, the great revolution in wall coverings came with the fashion for silks or damasks (reversible fabrics of silk or linen with a woven patterned surface), so that hangings of these materials could be bought by the yard and applied to any wall space, fixed to the frames that made up the architecture of each wall of the room. Between 1679 and 1683 the ante-chamber to the Queen's Bedroom at Ham House was fitted with 'foure pieces of blewe Damusk, impaned and bordered wth. blew velvet embroidered with gould and fringed'.

20 Detail of a wall hanging imitating panelling, about 1600. Painted for the upper room of The Lockers, Hemel Hempstead, Hertfordshire. Tempera on canvas panels, painted. VAM W.41-1952.

21 Wall hanging, about 1720. Made for Jenkyn Place, Bentley, Hampshire. Distemper on canvas, painted and possibly partly printed. [h. 152cm]. VAM. Anonymous loan.

22 Leather panel, about 1670. Attributed to Martinus Van den Heuvel the Younger, owner of the gilt leather firm, Compagnie van Goudleermaken of Amsterdam. Embossed leather with metallic finish, paint and coloured glazes. [h. 86cm]. VAM W.67-1911.

23

23 The painted chamber, Gladstone's
Land, Edinburgh. The painted ceiling in
this upstairs room of a merchant's house
dates from 1617–20.

24

Wallpaper first appeared in England in the early sixteenth century in small printed sheets, but the technology developed so that longer lengths were being produced by the end of the seventeenth century. In John Houghton's *A Collection of Letters for the Improvement of Husbandry and Trade* of 1689 the author describes the older tradition of small sheets, but goes on, ' . . . there are some other done in Rolls in long sheets of thick paper made for the Purpose whose sheets are pasted together to be so long as the Height of a Room, and they are managed like Woolen hangings, and there is a great Variety, with curious Cuts, which are Cheap, and if kept from Wet, very lasting'. Wallpaper was sufficiently established that a tax was first imposed in 1712.

Above the wall-plate level in especially grand rooms, the frieze might be painted in the early sixteenth century; examples survive with rough but vigorous work in the antique style, but increasingly the frieze was a field garnished with plasterwork, which later extended to ceilings. After a period in the early sixteenth century when ceilings were decorated with wooden battens or ribs – filled, in the case of the royal palaces of Henry VIII, with decorative *all'antica* ornament in papier mâché or pressed leather – the fashion for plaster ceilings became popular after about 1570, with the first appearance of plaster ceilings with hanging pendants. These ceilings carried family heraldry and often emblematic devices, or representations of the months, the seasons or the worthies. A particularly rich tradition of lavishly painted, sometimes emblematic ceilings developed in Scotland between about 1570 and 1640, but there painted directly on to the wooden beams of the most important rooms in the house. By the mid-seventeenth century the taste had changed in both England and Scotland to the use of plasterwork for geometrically divided compartments, now usually banishing emblems in favour of wreaths of fruit and flowers and heavy classical mouldings.

25

4. Furnishings

Sixteenth-century inventories, recording all the movable goods of the house at a critical point in its history (usually the death of the owner), list a variety of objects, but with a proliferation throughout the house which suggests that things were much moved around. Furniture at this time, predominantly of oak, fulfilled the basic requirements of seating, surfaces for eating and storage, with a sufficiency of soft furnishings in the form of cushions and table carpets to render the surfaces more comfortable and luxurious. Fairly simple wooden furniture (items such as framed chests and cupboards, gate-leg tables and panel-backed chairs) remained the staple furnishing of modest houses throughout the seventeenth century, individualized and regionalized by the use of distinctive geometric motifs, or sometimes with biblical or other

24 The great chamber, Canons Ashby, Northamptonshire. The plaster ceiling was installed shortly after 1632.

25 Armchair, about 1540. Carved and joined oak. VAM W.39-1920.

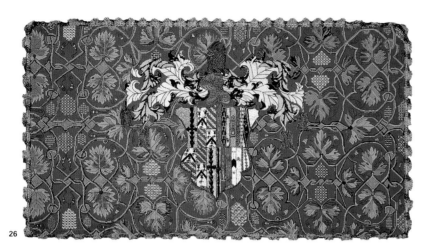

inscriptions. Furniture with leather seats and backs was a feature of the mid-century period. Walnut furniture became fashionable for the wealthier classes, as did, by the 1670s, furniture covered with marquetry: a decorative veneer applied to the surface and made up of pieces of wood and perhaps other materials, like ivory or bone, to form a pictorial or patterned mosaic.

For seating, the seventeenth century saw a great increase in upholstered furniture, with whole sets of chairs, footstools and benches being commissioned, notably accompanying a state bed. Indeed, in the decades after

1660, so expensive and dominant were the upholstered items in a room of state that the upholsterer in effect became the designer of the interior furnishings as a whole. High-backed cane chairs were often used in dining rooms, halls and vestibules where people waited and in everyday living parlours.

26 Cushion cover with the arms of Sandys and Windsor, impaling vines, probably 1550s. Linen canvas embroidered with silk and metal thread in long-armed cross and tent stitches, laid and couched work. VAM T.51-1978.

27 Draw-table, about 1600. Made in England, though the design of the bulbous legs is Flemish and German in origin. Inlaid and carved oak, sycamore, holly and bog-oak. VAM 384-1898.

28 Gate-leg table, about 1700–10. Elm, turned and joined. VAM W.37-1938.

One significant area of textile production – that of embroidery – remained firmly within the domestic sphere. The appropriateness of the task of embroidery at home is stressed from the late sixteenth century onwards in conduct books for women and it was a task carried out, it seems, by women of all classes, from Mary, Queen of Scots and Bess of Hardwick to the daughters of the professional class. While much sixteenth-century embroidery was for clothes and hangings, in the seventeenth century boxes, caskets and mirror surrounds were worked. Mirrors are especially interesting, given their expense (home-produced mirrors were of poor quality and the best were imported from Venice) and their association with the sin of vanity. Surrounding the mirror with an uplifting embroidered narrative or image therefore turned the object into a moral lesson for maker and viewer alike. Particularly popular during the reign of Charles II were images of the King and Queen flanking mirrors.

29 Chair, 1695–1705. Made in England. Carved and turned walnut with cane seat and back. VAM W.35-1936.

30 Armchair, about 1670. Probably made in France for Ham House, London. Beech, carved, gilded and silvered with traces of coloured glazes. VAM HH.81:1-1948.

31 Mirror frame, 1660–80. The king and queen represented are probably Charles II and Catherine of Braganza, his wife. Border of satin embroidered with silk and metal thread; framed in wood painted to imitate lacquer. VAM 351-1886.

TEXTILES FOR THE HOME

Sara Pennell

The importance that people in the sixteenth and seventeenth centuries accorded to textiles as domestic furnishings is captured by William Harrison's observation in 1577 that even artificers and farmers now furnished their 'beds with tapestry and silk hangings, and their tables with carpets and fine napery'. These had been the traditional prerogatives of the noble household. Their spread down the social scale was visible evidence of an improvement in living standards among the middling groups in the population.

Textiles had a vital practical function at a time when interiors consisted of timber floors, wainscoted walls and rooms often lacking hearths. Practicality did not, however, preclude decoration and luxury. The most exclusive (often imported) fabrics, like cloth-of-gold, remained the preserve of kings and courtiers. Yet by the close of the sixteenth century a growing indigenous industry using skills drawn from continental Europe was producing a versatile range of furnishing textiles – light woollens and wool-linen mixes, such as

32. Hangings on a bed at Doddington Hall, Lincolnshire, 1680. Crewelwork.

dornixes, dyed with novel dyestuffs. Carpets from Persia and Turkey introduced yet more colour and pattern, as did Indian painted fabrics ('pintadoes'), the precursors of the chintzes and calicoes that flourished a century later.

How these textiles were used illustrates the flexibility of furnishings in the era before fixed seat upholstery and wallpapers. The elaborately embroidered cushions that softened wooden seat furniture, the carpets that dressed tables – all were eminently mobile. Even costly tapestries like Charles I's Mortlake sets travelled from palace to palace, as occasion demanded. Domestic textiles were 'mobile' in another sense, too, as one of the major forms of wealth bequeathed down the generations. Surviving crewelwork bed curtains made by Abigail Pett may indeed be the set belonging to the 'complete bed' that she left in her will, dated 1706.

Needleworking was considered an appropriate 'knowledge' to be learned by women who aspired to good housewifery, not least because its products were considered

33. *The Somerset House Conference*, **about 1604. Painted by an unknown artist. The scene shows the signing of an Anglo-Spanish peace treaty in Somerset House, London, a royal property. Turkish carpets cover the table and floor, and Flemish tapestries the walls. The delegates are seated on upholstered chairs. Oil on canvas. National Portrait Gallery, London.**

valuable ornaments to the domestic environment. However, considerable application was needed to embroider a complete set of bed curtains. Sometimes it deserted even the most dedicated needlewoman. In 1657 the wealthy lawyer Heneage Finch reported that his wife had nearly completed a set of bed curtains, but as for the matching carpet and seating, 'I should despayr of seeing an end of them.' Such industry notwithstanding, domestically produced textiles were often used alongside ready-made products throughout the Tudor–Stuart period. The commercial availability of popular designs in books, prints and ready-drawn patterns sold by booksellers also meant that motifs used by professional embroiderers were accessible to domestic needleworkers.

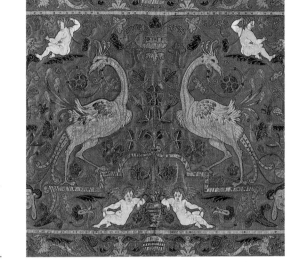

35. Detail of a cushion cover, about 1550–1600. Perhaps made for a stool or chair. Woven silk satin ground, with applied work in velvet, cloth-of-silver and silk; embroidered details in silk, metal thread and sequins. VAM T.22-1947.

36. Tapestry showing the story of Vulcan and Venus, 1620–5. Woven in the Mortlake tapestry factory, London. The design is taken from 16th-century Brussels tapestries. From a set made for Charles, Prince of Wales, later Charles I. Woven wool, silk and metal thread. [h. 453cm]. VAM T.170-1978.

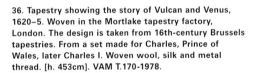

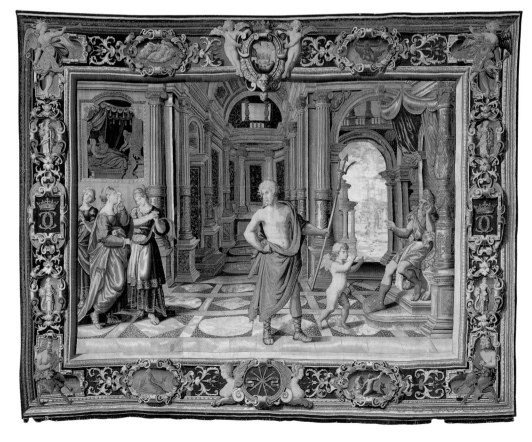

34. Bed hanging, 1680–1700. Embroidered by Abigail Pett, who put her name on an associated valance. The foliage influenced by imported Indian textiles. Embroidered in crewel wool on a linen and cotton ground. [h. 195.6cm]. VAM T.13-1929.

5. Buying in town

Shopping for goods for the home and personal attire was one of the primary attractions of the great urban centres. London led the way, but many provincial cities and towns also increased their trade in goods hugely in this period. Some places, like Canterbury, that had been great centres of pilgrimage in earlier times needed to diversify after the Reformation and became places of leisure by the end of the seventeenth century, attracting local wealthy gentry and the nobility. Through great centres of trade, goods from around the world became increasingly the common currency of luxury buying.

Sir Thomas Smith, scholar and political writer, remarked as early as 1549 that within the last 20 years perhaps a dozen haberdashers' shops in London had grown to such a number that 'from the towere to westminster alonge, everie streate is full of them; and their shoppes glisters and shine of glasses, as well lookinge as drinckinge, yea all mannor of vesselles of the same stuffe, painted cuses, gaye daggers, knives, swordes, and girdles'. The building of the Gresham's (later named the Royal) Exchange in 1578 and then the New Exchange, built as a speculative venture by Sir Robert Cecil in 1609, created the equivalent of shopping malls in Elizabethan and Jacobean London, with many small booths gathered together under one roof. In other parts of the city it is noticeable that retail spaces became larger at this time. The capital was of course the chief distribution point for foreign goods, and for a considerable time there was much anxiety about the unfavourable balance of trade. Elizabeth I's chief minister William Cecil noted the 'excess of silkes . . . of wyne and spice' (wine imports quadrupled during Elizabeth's 45-year reign) and believed that their promotion was a way of 'consent to the robbery of the realm'.

Provincial cities like Gloucester became suppliers for a large network of part-time shops in rural areas within a 24–30 kilometre radius, as well as serving the local gentry who visited to buy. While Gloucester depended heavily on Bristol for foreign imports, it is true to say that London fashions in a whole range of goods, from clothes to domestic fixtures and the ordering of funerary monuments, were especially dominant by 1700, with the result that it is more difficult to characterize and identify regional styles of goods than it is from the period around 1500.

37

38

37 Casting bottle, about 1540–50. Made in England by an unknown goldsmith, using the maker's mark of a cusped I. For the keeping and sprinkling of perfumed water. Silver, chased, embossed and engraved. VAM 451-1865.

38 Detail of a fringe, about 1600–30. Made in Italy or possibly England. A trimming for upholstered furniture. Silk, gold and silver thread. [w. 8.5cm]. VAM T.270-1965.

39

By 1700 shops were being designed with interior architectonic features like stage sets, and glazed windows allowed a view from the outside. There were anxieties about the increasing popularity of shopping turning it from a necessary activity to one of leisure. Women were seen as especially prone to the temptations of shopping, particularly where clothes were concerned. A character in Ben Jonson's play *Epicene* warns another of the danger of marriage and of women's lust for consumer goods: 'She must have that rich gown for such a great day, a new one for the next, a richer for the third; be served in silver; have the chamber filled with a succession of grooms, footmen, ushers and other messengers, besides embroiderers, jewellers, tire-women, sempsters [seam-stresses], feathermen, perfumers.' As so often in a patriarchal society, women got the blame for a general unease about society's indulgences. It is interesting, too, that the desire for the latest fashion in dress heads the list of these 'sins' of excess.

40

---

39 Tobacco box, with London hallmarks for 1655–6. Mark of 'IS'. The luxury of tobacco stimulated expensive accessories such as this box. Silver, engraved. [h. 2.4cm]. VAM M.695-1926.

40 Trade card for the Blue Paper warehouse, Aldermanbury, London, about 1710. The proprietor, Abraham Price, stands at the door of his shop. The process of wallpaper printing is depicted at the top left. Engraving. Bodleian Library.

6. Dress codes

Like extravagant building, excessive attention and expenditure on dress invoke the threat of severe punishment in the Bible, which was the authoritative support for much of the high moral tone taken by the critics of luxury. One of their major anxieties concerned the possible assumption of habits of dress above the station of the individual. The sumptuary laws of sixteenth-century England sought to control dress by regulating who could wear what fabric, what colour, in what place and on what occasion. While the repeated issuing of these laws throughout the century suggests that they were difficult to enforce, they do remind us that apparel and its decoration were significant means of understanding rank and status in public places.

In the last proclamation of Elizabeth I's reign, issued in 1597, expensive fabrics were predictably reserved for the upper ranks of society: for men, satin, damask, grosgrain (a coarse fabric invariably containing some silk) and taffeta in hose and doublet were forbidden to those under the degree of a gentleman bearing arms, for instance. Interestingly too, significant accoutrements signifying power were also to be controlled: lace mixed with gold or silver, spurs, swords, rapiers, daggers, wood knives, hangers, buckles or studs of gilt could be worn only by the son of a baron, or higher. Many of the items listed here remind us of the constant government concern about public order and with keeping weapons out of the hands of the lower classes. Court officials, of whatever origin, were exempted from most of these constraints. Most revealingly, those under the degree of baron were forbidden to wear woollen cloth made out of the country, suggesting an eye on the need to control the import of foreign fashions. That the sumptuary laws were governed by political expediency is quite apparent from the fact that after 1600 they ceased to be renewed.

Sixteenth-century fashionable dress was dominated by foreign styles, especially at the royal court, where foreign ambassadors were expected to comment on appearances and attest to the richness of apparel being superior to that of their own countries. The pointed gable hood, which was a familiar element of elite female dress in the first half of the century and one that was distinctively English, was sometimes supplanted by the fashionable French hood; this was rounded, set further back and followed the shape of the head. Yet dress was customized to some extent through the choice of material and a love of certain motifs; floral motifs, often emblematic of love or of loyalty to a particular patron, constantly reappeared in English fashions throughout the sixteenth century.

Dress was characterized by the emphasis of certain prominent features – the framing of the head and hands by elaborate necklines, ruffs and cuffs – yet by the denial of the basic body shape. In the case of men, the physical bulk of the upper body was expressed by the wide-shouldered fashions of the first half of the century. The shoulders were narrowed by tighter-fitting doublets in the

41

second half of the century, when male fashions increasingly emphasized (even fetishized) the legs. For women, clothes divided the body into a series of geometric shapes, particularly the triangle of the bodice and the wide skirt, emphasized towards the mid-century by a triangular opening at the front to reveal the underskirt beneath. While the basic shapes of major garments often stayed in fashion for 20 or 30 years, particular additions to dress (what we would now term accessories) put the wearer in the height of fashion. Thus jewellery, hats, gloves and fans, for example, often help to date the dress in a portrait because these things would be especially sensitive to the latest influences from home and abroad.

Clothes for both sexes were covered with surface detail. From about 1510 outer garments were often slashed to reveal the linen beneath. Renaissance ornament, particularly patterns of the moresque design, was applied to underskirts, in the black patterned edging of necklines and the cuffs to shirts, and on the front of the doublet. Occasionally aspects of male and female dress influenced each other. In the 1560s and 1570s women sometimes wore tall, sober hats after the male fashion, and the bodices of their dresses were

41 *Margaret Laton,* about 1620. Probably painted in London by Marcus Gheeraerts the Younger (*see 2:27 for her jacket*). Oil on oak panel. VAM E.214-1994.

sometimes influenced by the fastenings of male doublets. Men in the 1580s wore earrings and wore their hair longer. Spanish fashions were especially dominant in about 1600 and encouraged the apogee of elaborate dress for men, with wide, baggy breeches known as 'slops', ruffs (or more commonly by this time starched high collars) framing the head and cutting it off from the body, and a wealth of trimmings and ornament.

Dress took a different turn from about the 1620s, when French influence began to dominate, especially through the leading role played by Charles I's queen, Henrietta Maria. The contours of clothes were softened, plain satins of duller colours were now in evidence and the spiky lace of earlier times gave way to soft bobbin lace. All this reflected a move away from the use of highly patterned materials echoing contemporary heraldry, as a sign of rank and class, towards a sense of demeanour, of knowing how to conduct oneself in these looser fashions to convey a sign of good breeding and education in appropriate manners. Men abandoned shoes with elaborate pompons for boots made of soft Cordoba leather and fashionable women dressed with a careful sense of disorder that was positively *déshabillé*.

42 *Anne Erskine, Countess of Rothes and her daughters, Lady Margaret and Lady Mary Leslie*, 1626. By George Jamesone. Oil on canvas. Scottish National Portrait Gallery.

43 *A woman, possibly Elizabeth Capell, the Countess of Caernarvon*, 1653-7. By Richard Gibson. Watercolour on vellum, put down on pasteboard. Fruitwood frame. VAM P.15-1926.

LORD AND LADY CLAPHAM

Susan North

Lord and Lady Clapham are accurate and unique documents of dress history; their clothes are perfect miniatures of fashions of the 1690s. Such elaborate and expensive dolls were not children's toys. They were made for the amusement of older girls and women, in the same manner as the 'baby houses' or doll houses of the late seventeenth century.

Lady Clapham's formal garments include a mantua, a type of woman's gown introduced in the 1670s. It is made from white Chinese silk damask trimmed with lace and worn with a matching petticoat. Underneath she wears linen petticoats and boned stays, which give her torso the tubular shape fashionable in the 1690s. Lord Clapham's coat, waistcoat and breeches represent the three-piece outfit introduced by Charles II in the 1660s. Over the next three centuries this ensemble would evolve into the modern business suit. At this period the three garments were not expected to match. Lord Clapham's coat is made of scarlet English wool; his waistcoat and breeches of white silk, probably French, elaborately patterned in silver thread.

Both Lord and Lady Clapham have nightgowns made from silk imported from China. The nightgown was a new item of dress added to the wardrobes of wealthy men and women in the 1670s; it was not worn to bed, but for relaxing in private at home. These

informal gowns were Western variations of the Japanese kimono, whose influence in Europe came through the Dutch East India Company. The man's nightgown is almost an exact copy of the kimono in cut and construction, being a simple T-shaped garment. It would have been

44. Lord and Lady Clapham in formal dress, about 1690–1700. Wood wrapped with wool, faces gessoed and painted, with wigs of human hair. [h. 55cm seated]. VAM T.846-1974, T.847-1974.

worn over the shirt and breeches. The gathers at the back neck and a tuck on either shoulder of Lady Clapham's nightgown illustrate the modifications made in order to accommodate the matching petticoat worn underneath.

What is exceptional about the dolls and their clothes is that they preserve many accessories that do not survive as full-sized garments, as well as illustrating the order in which the garments were worn. Lady Clapham's outfit even includes a mask of the sort worn at the masked balls that were so popular in the seventeenth and eighteenth centuries. Made of cardboard lined with vellum and covered with black silk, it was kept in place by means of a bead attached inside, which was held between the teeth.

45. Lady Clapham's mask. VAM T.846:T-1974.

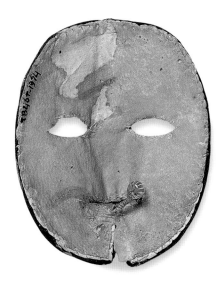

46. The back of Lady Clapham's mask. VAM T.846:T-1974.

47. Lady Clapham in her
shift, stockings, garters,
shoes, underpetticoat
and 'pocket' (a separate
garment). VAM T.846:
A,B,C,G,H,I,J,K&L-1974.

48. Lord Clapham in his
shirt, stockings, garters,
shoes and breeches. VAM
T.847:A,B,F,G,H,I&J-1974.

49. Lady Clapham's
nightgown.
VAM T.846:N-1974.

50. Lord Clapham's
nightgown.
VAM T.847:N-1974.

In the later years of the seventeenth century rigidity again entered women's fashion with the wearing of boned bodices, then boned stays and, in the 1690s, the introduction of the bustle at the back of the gown. But an informal looseness persisted, especially with the emergence of the mantua in the 1670s, a loose gown that draped over the rigid foundation garments. Men's fashion also became more formalized, yet in a comfortable and malleable way that was to introduce a basic convention lasting down to modern times. The development of the ensemble of a vest or waistcoat (first knee-length, but later raised to waist-high) along with knee breeches and top coat became the origin of the three-piece suit. Both sexes enjoyed more casual wear.

These developments broadly followed the fashions set in France, despite the attempts of Charles II to develop a distinctively English style of dress for men in the 1660s, employing exclusively English materials. Yet for all the powerful influence exercised by French modes, by the start of the eighteenth century British fashion, especially for men, had a reputation for sobriety compared with the most extravagant of continental fashion. By 1722 a travel guide was to point out that 'the dress of the English is like the French but not so gaudy; they generally go plain but in the best cloths and stuffs'. It added that 'they wear embroidery and laces on their cloathes on solemn days, but they don't make it their daily wear, as the French do'.

This picture of changing fashions tells but one half of the story, for the expense of luxurious apparel meant that there was a thriving trade in second-hand clothes and the refashioning of fabrics at all times. Some clothes were passed on through wills; items trimmed with fur in particular often headed the list of gifts to family, friends or business associates. In her will of 1531 Margaret Heron, of Hackney (now part of London, but then in the county of Middlesex), left her 'gowne of blacke satten furrid' to her son John and her kirtles (also gowns) to her sister, god-daughter and other women she knew. At this time, immediately before the worst excesses of stripping churches of their furnishings during the Reformation, people often left expensive fabrics to the Church, so Margaret Heron also left a gown of tawny velvet to make a vestment or cope. References in the Assize records to the theft of clothing, not just of expensive items but of fine linen from washing lines, testify to an unofficial circulation of goods. Fabric could also be reworked and refashioned if its original expense was worth the effort; goldsmiths were known to buy materials with gold thread, or silver and gold trimmings, to recover the precious metal they contained.

51

51 A pair of stays, 1660–70. Probably made in England. This under-garment was essential for the flat-fronted female silhouette, yet the material, sleeves and front lacing suggest that it was meant to be seen when dressed informally. Pink watered silk, backed with linen, stiffened with whalebone and trimmed with pink silk ribbons. VAM T.14-1951.

52

7. The outside world

One of the messages conveyed by items of dress depicted in sixteenth- and seventeenth-century portraits was the presence of the wearer in public or private spaces; such signals would have been clearly understood at the time but are now of a subtlety that is lost to us. The wearing of one glove, for example, and the carrying of the other may have indicated that the sitter was about to move from home to a public place. A more obvious, yet still domestic, way of representing the outside world in portraits was to suggest the presence of a garden in the background and to one side of the picture. In the early sixteenth century most gardens, even at great houses, were relatively small; they tended to be seen as private enclosures and might lead to walks along walls, give access to ancillary buildings or even the means for the owner to reach the local church, as at Thornbury Castle near the Bristol Channel, built by the Duke of Buckingham in the years before his execution in 1521. In his house at Chelsea, Sir Thomas More had a garden retreat for study and contemplation.

54

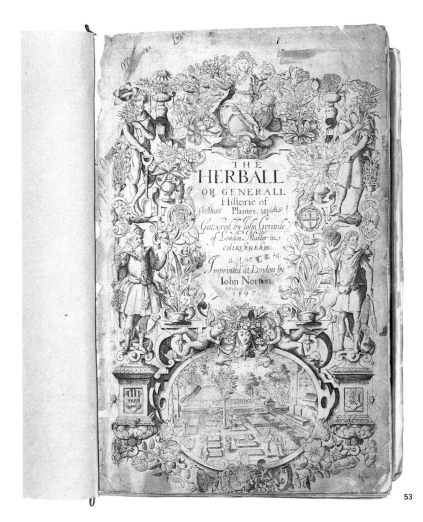

53

Early Tudor enclosed gardens often had knot gardens, arbours, mounds from which to view the surroundings, and topiary. The garden was a source of pleasure, but also of food and herbs for medicinal use and for the banishment of smells from the house – hence their portrayal in books known as herbals, a sort of treatise on plants with advice on their usefulness. By the later sixteenth century gardens were often larger, spread out from one or more sides of a great house and were increasingly designed at the same time as the building, or certainly envisaged alongside it. This was the period when the first distinctive 'garden' side to the house, distinct in architectural character from the main entrance front, began to appear, sometimes with a terrace or loggia linking the two. Garden buildings at this period often explored new ideas in building design; small structures in ingenious geometric shapes might serve as places of retreat or as 'banqueting houses' where the owner and guests took sweetmeats after the main meal of the day. Ingenuity extended also to water features.

---

52 Wedding suit, 1673. Made for James, Duke of York (later James II and VII) for his wedding to Mary of Modena. Wool embroidered with silver and silver-gilt thread and lined with red silk. VAM T.711-1995.

53 *The Herball, or Generall Historie of Plantes* by John Gerarde, 1597 Printed by Edmund Bollifant and published by John Norton. Engraving. VAM 86.F.92.

54 Detail of *Sir Thomas More, his family and descendants*, 1593–4. Probably by Rowland Lockey after an earlier painting by Hans Holbein. This is thought to represent Sir Thomas More's garden at his house in Chelsea, created in the 1520s, with his brick study or retreat. Watercolour on vellum, stuck on card. VAM P.15-1973.

124

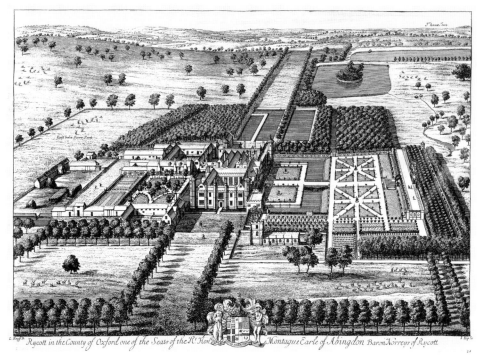

55

56

Greater formality appeared with the seventeenth century, inspired by Italian example. The century's concept of formality meant that the act of looking at the garden – already significant in the sense that great sixteenth-century houses often had rooftop walks – became more important than the exploration of it. Gardens were viewed from the first-floor state apartment. Vistas were created towards garden features. The knot gardens of the sixteenth century gave way to the terraced *parterres* of the seventeenth, some of these known as *parterres de broderie*, filled with flowers, grass and gravel, and edged with box, to create flowing patterns. Garden statuary, sometimes original works imported from Italy, but more often copies of antique sculpture, became central features of planned garden design. Towards the end of the seventeenth century long, formal canals and large, circular basins became common, influenced by French and Dutch example. More elaborate waterworks, such as fountains and cascades, were also popular. Older gardens were modernized, sometimes using remaining parts of a medieval moat to turn a once defensive necessity into a pleasurable, reflective surface.

Also significant is the way in which the concept of the garden was extended into the public sphere, as public gardens became places of resort and encounter. Hyde Park in London was still used for hunting at the time of James I and VI, but during the reign of his son, Charles I, it became a parade ground for the coaches of the wealthy. At this time the Mulberry Gardens in the royal parks of London and the commercially run Spring Gardens were intended as places of simple natural pleasures, but became places of scandal.

It was relayed to the Earl of Strafford in 1634 that:

> The Bowling in the Spring Garden was by the King's Command put down for one day . . . continual bibbling and drinking of wine all day long under the trees, two or three quarrels every week. It was grown scandalous and insufferable; besides, my Lord Digby being reprehended for striking in the King's garden, he answered that he took it for a common bowling place where all paid money for their coming in.

In 1661 John Evelyn went to see the New Spring Garden at Lambeth, also a commercial entertainment, which he described as 'a pretty contrived plantation'. This garden formed the beginnings of the famous establishment later called the Vauxhall Gardens, described by a foreign visitor in 1710 as consisting 'entirely of avenues and covered walks . . . and green huts, in which one can get a glass of wine, snuff and other things, although everything is very dear and bad'.

55 The water garden, Westbury Court, Gloucestershire, 1696–1705.

56 *Rycote House*. Plate from *Britannia Illustrata*, 1707. By Johannes Kip and Leonard Knyff. The Tudor house has been given new formal gardens and the moat turned into a water feature. Engraving. Corporation of London.

57

8. Coffee houses as places of debate

Other places of public resort were the coffee houses that were proliferating by 1700, a new venue of indoor social interaction to supplement the long-established inns and taverns. One of the earliest known examples opened in Oxford in 1650. Most provincial towns had one or two by the end of the century, but in London the numbers ran to hundreds. In 1719 they were described by a French traveller as 'extremely convenient. You have all manner of news there; you have a good fire, which you may sit by as long as you please; you have a dish of coffee; you meet your friends for the transaction of business, and all for a penny, if you don't care to spend more.'

This novel environment was, for its frequenters, an alternative to domestic social life, and a new range of objects emerged to serve the pursuits that went on there. Coffee pots and coffee dishes sat alongside newspapers and tobacco pipes. The reputation of the coffee house for serious discussion made it the most significant debating place of the early eighteenth century. The poet Oliver Goldsmith described how he saw clergymen writing their sermons there; the journalist Joseph Addison sat in them writing for the *Spectator*; and the painter William Hogarth's father set up a coffee house where Latin was to be spoken. They were predominantly, given the exclusion of women from public political debate, male preserves. They represent, however, the mark of a fundamental shift in British society. In 1500 the church remained the most obvious place of public assembly. Throughout the seventeenth century, as the voices of religious dissent sought to control the excesses of what they saw as a tyrannical monarchy, the Puritan chapel became the focus of debate and 'the citadel of seventeenth-century freedoms'. By 1700 it was the coffee house that had become, in the words of Abbé Prévost, the 'seat of English liberty', where discussion of everything from politics to social mores was open to a mix of classes and religious denominations.

57 Detail of *Arthur, 1st Baron Capel and his family*, about 1639. By Cornelius Johnson (Cornelis Jonson van Ceulen I). This garden at Little Hadham, Hertfordshire, was laid out in the 1630s. Oil on canvas. National Portrait Gallery, London.

58 *A London coffee house*, about 1700. By an anonymous artist. Body-colour. The British Museum.

CHAPTER 5

What was new?

JOHN STYLES

1. Unnecessary foreign wares

When in 1549, in his *Discourse of the Common Weal of this Realm of England*, Sir Thomas Smith railed against the haberdashers' shops that had recently proliferated in London, his anger centred on the attractive imported goods they stocked in such profusion – 'French or Milan caps, glasses, daggers, swords, girdles, and such things.' Many of these goods were, Smith complained, mere fripperies, made from cheap materials – paper, pins, needles, knives, hats, caps, brooches, buttons, laces, gloves, tables, playing cards, puppets, hawks' bells, earthen wares – yet in importing them, the kingdom wasted its resources. England was 'overburdened with unnecessary forrayn wares', things 'that we might ether clene spare, or els make them within oure owne realme'.

The annoyance expressed by Smith at the rising tide of foreign imports exposes an ambivalence in English attitudes towards innovation during the Tudor period. On the one hand, it betrays a suspicion that many of the small, often decorated consumer goods being imported in ever-increasing quantities were wasteful and unnecessary extravagances. On the other hand, it reveals a dismay at England's inability to make such goods and resentment at the lost opportunities that their import represented for English workers. Disapproval of superfluous novelties was to persist throughout the rest of the Tudor and Stuart period, though it did little to prevent them being bought and enjoyed in growing quantities. By contrast, dismay at the country's dependence on foreigners to supply those novelties became an important force propelling innovation in design and the decorative arts.

Innovation in high-design goods in the sixteenth and seventeenth centuries was mainly a matter of imports and import substitution – the long drawn-out process by which the British learned to make decorative goods that were already familiar as imports, but required techniques and materials they had previously been unable to master. Britain was artistically and industrially

2

1 Uncut playing cards, about 1500. French. Card printed from woodblocks and hand-coloured. VAM E.988-1920.

2 German stoneware pot with English mounts, about 1550–60. Stoneware with silver-gilt mounts. VAM 2119-1855.

3 *John Rose, the Royal Gardener, presenting Charles II with the first pineapple grown in England*, 1787. By Thomas Hewart after a 17th-century painting at Houghton Hall attributed to Henry Danckerts. Pineapples originated in South America. Oil on canvas. VAM HH.191-1948.

backward by the standards of her continental neighbours. Innovation characteristically involved an extended process whereby goods were initially imported in their indigenous foreign forms, then tailored by their overseas makers to British tastes, then copied crudely in Britain and finally manufactured proficiently by the British. This broad sequence can be observed across a whole range of decorative goods, from German stoneware jugs to Indian decorated cottons.

The fact that innovation in design and the decorative arts came mainly from abroad should come as no surprise to us. After all, this was a period when almost every aspect of British life was becoming less provincial and more cosmopolitan. Take botanical knowledge. At the start of the sixteenth century the number of plant species known in Europe was approximately 500, not very different from the number known to the ancient Romans. By the time the English botanist John Ray compiled his catalogue of plants two centuries later nearly 20,000 species had been identified, mainly as a consequence of the European exploration of the extra-European world.

An equivalent process can be observed at work in the English language. The unsurpassed power and richness of the language used by Shakespeare and the translators of the King James Bible testify to a huge expansion in its vocabulary, the result of borrowings from Greek and Latin, from French, Italian and Dutch. As in design and the decorative arts, there were those who resented foreign imports. They wanted new words to be coined exclusively from English roots. But the poet Philip Sidney, writing at the end of the sixteenth century, defended these linguistic borrowings as a form of creative eclecticism that ultimately strengthened the English language. 'Some will say it is a mingled language. And why not,' he went on, 'so much the better, taking the best of both.'

The same could have been said of foreign innovations in design and the decorative arts. The British, eager to acquire new kinds of high-design goods that came from abroad, but resentful at the scale of imports, endeavoured to make the same goods themselves. More often than not, the initial intention was simply to produce British copies of foreign products. After all, copying and imitation had few negative connotations at this period. Originality, in its uncompromising modern sense, was not necessarily prized. Yet the mix of skills and raw materials, ideas and tastes that prevailed in Britain and its colonies often demanded adaptations that amounted to substantial innovations in themselves. Silver teapots, wine glasses made from lead glass, Christopher Wren's London churches – all these reworked elements that originally came from abroad into things that came to be regarded as distinctively English.

2. Spurs to innovation

Innovation in design and the decorative arts faced many obstacles in the sixteenth and seventeenth centuries. Politicians, as we have seen, worried about excessive imports of unnecessary trifles. Moralists feared that an inordinate interest in new and beautiful things would divert people's attention from God, or, worse still, seduce them into worshipping God in the wrong way. Established manufacturers and their workers made strenuous efforts to prevent both the introduction of new goods that might threaten their livelihoods and the settlement of immigrants with new skills. In an age that set great store by precedent and custom, it was hard to shake people from their established likes and dislikes. Furniture and textiles might be prized as much for their associations with stability, order and hierarchy as for being new, fashionable and up-to-date.

Yet novelty, in certain guises, was attractive to many; this was not confined to kings and their courtiers, who, in an age of competitive royal magnificence, could hardly avoid monitoring the ever-changing extravagances of foreign courts. It was a hunger for fashionable clothes that drove the sister of a humble Lancashire clergyman, Adam Martindale, to London against her parents' wishes in the 1620s. In explanation, her brother pointed out that 'freeholders' daughters were then confined to their felts, petticoats and waistcoats, cross handkerchiefs about their necks, and white cross clothes upon their heads, with coifs under them wrought with black silk or worsted'. He concluded, with more than a hint of irritation, 'these limitations I suppose she did not very well approve'. Manufacturers were well aware of the popular appetite for novelty. The historian Thomas Fuller explained how the use of a new name could stimulate sales of the colourful Norwich-made worsted cloths popular among the 'middling sort' of the population in the mid-seventeenth century. When particular designs of cloth 'begin to tire of sale', customers' interest could be 'quickened with a new name'. Not surprisingly, novelties introduced in one material were quickly copied in another, like the multi-coloured decorative motifs that appeared on large Staffordshire earthenware dishes about 1670, mimicking recent developments in the decoration of dishes made from both tin-glazed earthenware and pewter.

4 Dish decorated with the figure of a mermaid, 1670–89. Made by Thomas Toft in Staffordshire. Earthenware, lead-glazed, with trailed slip decoration. [diam. 44cm]. VAM 299-1869.

Moreover, the arguments against innovation offered by the enemies of novelty, both religious and secular, did not go uncontested. New inventions designed to bring about improvements in material life were consistent with God's purpose, argued the farmer and inventor Cressy Dymock in 1651. 'The reformation of states in civil affairs for the most part, is not compassed without violence and disturbances: but inventions make all men happy without either injury or damage to any one single person. Furthermore, new inventions are as it were new creations, and imitations of God's own works.' Inventions like printing, clocks and gunpowder, which had been unknown to the ancient Romans, were cited as evidence of the superiority of the modern over the ancient world.

A belief in the human capacity for intellectual innovation was fundamental to the new kind of experimental science that flourished in seventeenth-century Britain, notably in the work of Isaac Newton and Robert Boyle. One of the most influential statements of this belief was Francis Bacon's demand that God's works should be studied in order to achieve a 'knowledge of causes, and secret motions of things; and the enlarging of the bounds of human empire, to the effecting of all things possible'. The Royal Society, which was founded in 1660 with this broad purpose in mind, was committed to securing practical benefits from advances in scientific knowledge.

Crucial to the establishment of the Royal Society was a patriotic desire for national advancement. Its founders hoped 'to render England the glory of the western world, by making it the seat of the best knowledge, as well as it may be the seat of the greatest trade'. In the sixteenth century Britain's rulers became increasingly receptive to the notion that they should take responsibility for 'the weal and advancement of the state'. As a result, governments began to give more active support to the establishment of new industries, especially those that would reduce imports and provide employment. From the middle of the sixteenth century the English government encouraged the settlement of Protestant refugees from continental Europe who possessed skills in short supply in England. 'We ought to favour the straungers from whome wee learned so great benifites,' argued one writer, 'because wee are not so good devisers as followers of others'. Government also granted monopoly privileges to entrepreneurs prepared to invest in new forms of manufacturing, which often included restrictions on competing imports.

6

These policies had considerable success. New kinds of decorative manufactures were established in England, including the making of colourful woollen cloths of the kind woven in the Low Countries, known as the 'new draperies'; silk fabrics in the Italian style; tin-glazed ceramics using the techniques of Italian majolica and Dutch delftware; and crystal glass in the Venetian manner. But the effects of government policies on innovation in the later sixteenth and early seventeenth centuries were far from consistent. Governments were as interested in raising revenue and placating vested interests as they were in reducing imports and promoting employment. Sometimes they refused monopoly privileges to successful innovators, as in the case of William Lee, the Nottinghamshire clergyman who invented the first hand-powered knitting machine in the 1580s.

Often state-sponsored attempts at import substitution failed, none more spectacularly than the scheme to have all English woollen cloth dyed prior to export, promoted in 1614 by Sir William Cockayne, an immensely wealthy merchant, financier and London alderman. Sometimes immigrant settlers failed to perform their allotted role of passing on their skills to natives, like the German swordsmiths who settled at Hounslow in the 1620s. Occasionally

5

5 Barometer, about 1700. Designed and made by Daniel Quare. Experiments in London and Holland during this period resulted in an improved vacuum, which helped to make barometers more reliable. Turned ivory, ebonized wood and engraved brass. [h. 103.5cm]. VAM W.64-1926.

6 Dish depicting Frederick, King of Bohemia, with his wife and children, about 1627. Made in Southwark, London. Frederick of Bohemia was the husband of Elizabeth, the daughter of James I and VI. Deposed from the Bohemian throne, he became a popular Protestant hero in England. Tin-glazed earthenware. VAM C.38-1928.

opposition to imports had the perverse consequence of inhibiting the introduction of promising new materials, like the ban imposed in 1581 on the import of logwood, the new dyestuff for blacks and blues from the Caribbean, which was unjustifiably condemned as 'false and deceitful'.

A variety of official efforts to encourage import substitution continued throughout the seventeenth century. But there were changes of emphasis. After the civil war the granting of monopoly privileges was restricted, because they had become an issue in the quarrel between King and Parliament. Henceforth, protection from competition was provided for a limited period only to those who could prove themselves to be innovators, under a system that was to become the basis of modern patent law. Towards the end of the Stuart era official support for British manufactures came to focus increasingly on tariffs and other trade controls that facilitated exports and restricted imports. By 1714 a situation had developed whereby most foreign manufactures were subject to heavy import tariffs – so high, in the case of France, that a legal import trade was virtually impossible. Moreover, the import of certain goods (Indian decorated cotton textiles and French alamode silks, for example) was prohibited. Imports of manufactured goods now began to stagnate and even started to decline.

3. How things were made

Innovation in design and the decorative arts was inextricably linked to changes in the ways things were made. At the start of the sixteenth century most people in Britain lived in the countryside and were engaged in agriculture in one way or another. For the majority, material possessions were few, and their meagre stock of manufactured goods was largely made by craftspeople in the local village or town. Indeed, many of the items they possessed – in particular textiles – were manufactured, at least in part, in their own homes for their own use. The wealthier sections of the population, especially the nobility and the gentry, owned many more objects made at a distance, including decorative luxuries from abroad, like linen damask tablecloths from the Low Countries and Italian silk velvet garments. Nevertheless, by the standards that would prevail at the end of the seventeenth century, their possessions were often sparse. The wealthy too relied heavily on craftspeople in their localities: in the 1470s the Eyres, a gentry family from Hassop in Derbyshire, obtained most of their woollen cloth from local weavers, fullers and dyers. Wool and flax were spun, and hangings and garments embroidered, by the women of such families and their servants. At all levels of society, households and localities displayed a marked degree of self-sufficiency, even when it came to decorative goods.

The manufacturing enterprises that produced goods for sale in the early sixteenth century tended to be very small. In the countryside, most consisted of a self-employed craftsperson – a tailor, a weaver or a shoemaker – who worked with the assistance of his family or an apprentice, using a few, simple tools. Even in London and other large towns, where more specialized manufacturing trades like goldsmithing might serve a regional or national market among the better-off, many master craftspeople worked single-handed. In an affluent London trade, like the making of pewter plates and drinking vessels, the vast majority of craftspeople employed no more than three workers. Only in the manufacture of woollen cloth, the single major export industry, were enterprises with large numbers of employees at all familiar, and then only in some rural areas. In parts of Suffolk, Essex and the West Country master clothiers put out wool to hundreds of spinners and yarn to scores of weavers to work up in their homes for a wage, often on a part-time basis.

7 Bowl, early 16th century.
Made in England or Flanders. Pewter.
VAM M.37-1945.

SKILLS FROM EUROPE, 1500–1600

Sara Pennell

Prior to 1500 the major ports and cities in England and Scotland accommodated small foreign populations, consisting mainly of merchants trading with continental Europe and immigrant craftspeople, chiefly employed in leather working, tailoring and brewing. This small-scale foreign presence grew dramatically during the sixteenth century. Religious persecution of continental Protestants was one impetus to immigration. French and Dutch Reformed churches were established in London after 1550. By 1571 there were perhaps 10,000 foreigners (or 'strangers' as they were called) in London alone, comprising 10 per cent of the city's population. But persecution alone does not account for the rise in such numbers. Continental craft techniques and skills were much coveted in England, particularly in areas like glassmaking, where indigenous products were crude and imported wares answered the demand for high-quality goods.

The English government actively promoted the settlement of skilled foreign artisans in certain trades. Dutch and Flemish weavers were recruited to settle in East Anglia and the south-east, where they boosted flagging textile industries by helping to develop light woollen-mix fabrics, the so-called 'New Draperies'. Jacomo Verzelini, a Venetian glassmaker who helped establish the Crutched Friars glasshouse in London, was also encouraged to stay and pass on his expertise. A 1574 royal grant gave him a 21-year monopoly over the English manufacture and supply of Venetian-style glasswares.

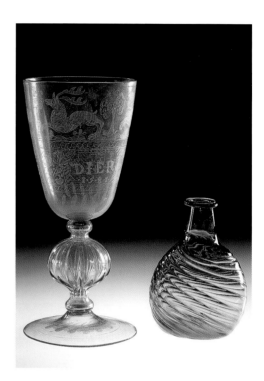

9. Left: wine glass, 1581. Probably made in London by Jacomo Verzelini, perhaps engraved by Anthony de Lysle. Engraved soda glass. [h. 21.2cm]. VAM C.523-1936. Right: flask, about 1580–1620. A typical example of native English glassmaking. Glass, mould-blown and 'wrythen' (twisted into a spiral). VAM C.1-1910.

8. *Londinium Feracissimi Angliae Regni Metropolis*. Map of the cities of London and Westminster from *Civitates Orbis Terrarum*, 1572. By Georg Braun and Franz Hogenberg. Printed in Antwerp. Bishopsgate, where many 'strangers' settled, is on the north-east edge of the built-up area shown on this map. Southwark is on the south bank of the River Thames. Woodcut and wash. Corporation of London.

The arrival of the 'strangers' was not universally welcomed. Fear of competition aroused hostility from the many guilds that controlled the organization of manufacturing in the City of London. They tried to restrict the places where immigrants could work and the people they could employ. To escape guild controls, many immigrants settled in areas like Bishopsgate and Southwark beyond the City walls, or pursued relatively 'young' trades such as printing, which as yet had little formal organization in London. Royal and aristocratic patronage likewise helped to protect foreign workers, such as the German armourers who settled in Greenwich.

It was primarily immigrants who enabled home-produced luxury goods like glasswares and armour to replace imports. Unlike native craftspeople, the 'strangers' were able to use new continental forms of ornament and design and brought with them technical skills (for example, in instrument making and printing) that were unmatched by most English artisans. The rate of immigration had peaked by the end of the sixteenth century, but immigrants continued to play an important role in high-design manufacturing throughout the seventeenth century. In 1607, for instance, the Goldsmiths' Company, the guild that represented native London goldsmiths, was still complaining that 'aliens and strangers [are] in better reputation and request than that of our own nation'.

11. Astronomical clock, dated 1588. Made in London by Francis Nowe, who was born in Brabant, the Netherlands. In 1571 he came to London, where he died in 1593. The earliest dated English clock. Engraved gilt-brass case, the movement a late 17th-century replacement. VAM M.39:1&2-1959.

12. Standing cup, with London hallmarks for 1611–12. Marked 'TvL' in monogram: made by an immigrant craftsman, perhaps by Thierry (Dierick) Luckemans. Silver-gilt, decorated with bands of applied wire (filigree), wire-work panels, chasing and engraving. VAM 5964:1&2-1859.

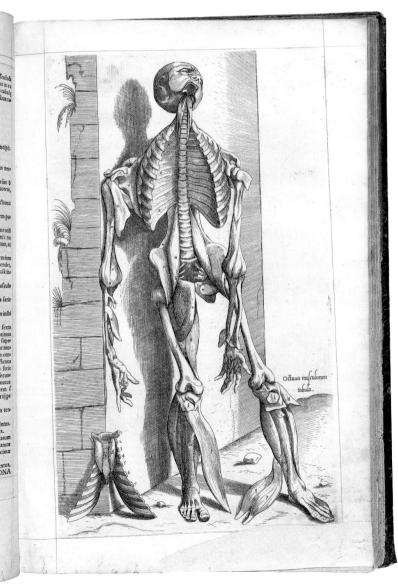

10. *Octava muscularum tabula*. Illustration in *Compendiosa totus anatomie delineatio*, 1545, written by Thomas Geminus, who was in England from about 1540. The text and illustrations taken from *De humani corporis fabrica* (Basel, 1543) by Andreas Vesalius. Printed in London by John Herford. Engraving. VAM RC.T.18.

JOHN DWIGHT

Robin Hildyard

In the seventeenth century the nationalistic desire to become independent of foreign imports such as Venetian glass, Chinese porcelain and German brown stoneware came to be combined with a new, more systematic approach to scientific research. After the failure of attempts to make stoneware at Woolwich and Southampton, it became apparent that only systematic experiment by an inspired chemist could unravel the complex secrets of high-fired ceramics.

The talents of John Dwight (about 1633–1703), the second son of an Oxfordshire yeoman, were recognized early. He studied law and chemistry at Oxford, later becoming legal adviser to the Church while pursuing his ceramic researches at Wigan. In 1672 he obtained a patent for 'Porcelane…as also…the stone ware vulgarly known as Cologne ware', and built a pottery at Fulham, then on the outskirts of London. His life of unceasing experimentation may be compared to those of

13. Left: *Lydia Dwight resurrected*, about 1674. John Dwight's daughter Lydia died at the age of six. Right: *John Dwight*, about 1673–5. Made by an unknown modeller at John Dwight's Fulham factory. Modelled and salt-glazed stoneware. VAM 1054-1871, 1053-1871.

Johann Friedrich Böttger, founder of the Meissen porcelain factory in Saxony in 1710, and Josiah Wedgwood, the eighteenth-century Staffordshire potter.

Initially Dwight hired experienced potters at Fulham and attempted to make every kind of pottery covered by his patent: tavern bottles and mugs, like those imported from Germany; porcelain and red stonewares, like those

imported from China; and his own innovative figures, which, with their dense body and tight-fitting glaze, had the capacity to simulate bronze. His stoneware bottles bore personalized medallions to compete with the newly invented glass wine bottles. Since the clay for his patented red stoneware was found only in Staffordshire, he allowed the Elers brothers there to make teapots, globular

14. *Neptune*, about 1673–5. Made by an unknown modeller at John Dwight's Fulham factory. Modelled stoneware with a wash to imitate bronze. VAM C.393-1920.

15. Three bottles. From left to right: about 1640–50, made in Woolwich; dated 1674, made in Southampton by William Killigrew; about 1675–80, made at John Dwight's Fulham factory. Salt-glazed stoneware. VAM C.1-1994, C.110-1995, C.59-1967.

16. Centre: 'gorge' mug, 17th century. Made in Westerwald, Germany. Left and right: fragments of two 'gorge' mugs, about 1675. Made at John Dwight's Fulham factory. Salt-glazed stoneware with applied and moulded decoration and partially painted in cobalt blue and manganese purple. VAM Circ.627-1926, 414/852-1885.

'gorges' for strong beer, and coffee and chocolate capuchines, but he also manufactured these objects himself at Fulham in refined brown and white stoneware.

Dwight's innovations represented major advances in European ceramics, especially his superior clay bodies incorporating Dorset clay and ground flint, and his use of marbled, splashed oxide, 'scratch-blue' and fine applied sprig decoration. For hot drinks, his stonewares proved vastly superior to soft lead-glazed English slipware and delftware. His innovations went on to form the basis for the great rise of the Staffordshire potteries in the eighteenth century. As for the magical porcelain, only his failure to find the vital China Stone in Cornwall prevented him from being the first European to crack the secret.

17. Centre: bottle, about 1685. [h. 17.2cm]. Left and right: two 'gorge' mugs, dated 1682 and about 1680–5. Made at John Dwight's Fulham factory. Salt-glazed stoneware with applied marbling and sprig-moulded decoration; silver mounts. VAM C.101-1938, 414/853-1885, 896-1905.

18. Left: capuchine and mug, about 1695. Made by David and John Philip Elers at Bradwell Wood, Staffordshire.
Right: capuchine and mug, about 1700. Made in the Dehua kilns in Fujian Province, China. Red stoneware and white porcelain. VAM C.100-1938, C.159-1932, 3588-1901, 3749-1901.

With the introduction of many entirely new and more sophisticated kinds of manufacturing in the later sixteenth and seventeenth centuries, the scale of industrial enterprises expanded. The rise of the large enterprise was most obvious in trades that required a concentration of expensive plant and machinery on a single site: the 70 water-powered paper mills that lined the rivers of south-east England and the Midlands by the late seventeenth century; the 26 London glass houses of the same period with their coal-fired furnaces; the potteries of Southwark and Lambeth, where colourful tin-glazed plates and bowls were made. Such plants could employ scores or, in exceptional cases, hundreds of workers. More than 200 people worked in the East India Company's shipyard at Blackwall Yard on the Thames in the 1620s. Setting up equipment like water wheels and coal-fired furnaces required a large outlay, but it is important to emphasize that the bulk of the work was still reliant on human eye and muscle. Potters' wheels were turned by foot; wood for ships was sawn by hand; glass was blown by mouth. These single-site establishments, moreover, were not the only kind of large enterprises producing decorative goods at this time. More common were businesses employing sometimes hundreds of people in their own homes under the putting-out system, increasingly as full-time workers. By the early eighteenth century they could be found in town and country, undertaking the manufacture of a vast range of decorative products – silks, linens and lace; stockings, hats and gloves; buttons, buckles and watches.

Most producers of decorative goods continued, however, to work on a small scale. Even in London, where the high-design trades requiring the greatest skills were concentrated, production was largely organized in workshops housing only a handful of workers. But these workshops did not operate in isolation. As Joseph Moxon noted in his *Mechanick Exercises* in 1678, 'One trade may borrow many Eminent Helps in work of another Trade.' In a number of trades,

20

19

19 Detail from an engraved invitation to a church service for members of the Goldsmiths' Company, 1701. This engraving does not provide an accurate depiction of a London goldsmith's workshop, but illustrates the range of activities that might be conducted there and the tools employed. Engraving. © The Worshipful Company of Goldsmiths.

specialist retailers abandoned production to concentrate on assembling an attractive array of goods for their customers from a variety of makers. Such were the upholders who emerged in the later seventeenth century to provide a comprehensive furnishing service for the homes of the wealthy. At the same time workshops in the high-design trades increasingly came to specialize in particular types of work, subcontracting some tasks to other workshops. The leading Restoration London goldsmith, Thomas Fowle, subcontracted gilding, engraving, planishing, burnishing and the making of jewellery, flatware, casters and chafing dishes. The practice was to become even more widespread in the eighteenth century, when it was claimed to give the London high-design trades an advantage over their continental competitors who had to rely on multi-skilled, non-specialist workers.

Guild controls in London generally proved ineffective against subcontracting, especially after the mid-seventeenth century. Most urban trades in the sixteenth and seventeenth centuries were organized in guilds, which policed entry into the trade and training for it. In London the number of guilds increased during this period, but despite their wealth and political influence, many of them exercised relatively little control over the aesthetic quality of the goods their members produced. In the late sixteenth and early seventeenth centuries the Goldsmiths' Company, for example, intermittently tried to make young workers produce a masterpiece to demonstrate their all-round command of the skills of the trade, a common guild requirement on the continent, but the policy appears to have been widely flouted and was abandoned in the 1630s.

20 *The East India Company's Yard at Deptford*, London, about 1660. By an unknown artist. Oil on canvas. © National Maritime Museum, London.

Increasing specialization in manufacturing at this time had other consequences. Households became less self-sufficient, with a decline in the amount of woollen and linen cloth made for the household's own use and a corresponding rise in purchases of an expanding range of ready-woven cloth. Yet at the same time women in wealthier households seem to have undertaken ever-more elaborate decorative needlework for domestic use, although they sometimes drew on the services of professional embroiderers. New forms of embroidery emerged, such as the sewing of figurative and narrative scenes on domestic objects like mirror surrounds, cushions and boxes.

21 *William Broderick, the King's Embroiderer*, 1614. By an unknown artist. Oil on panel. Wandsworth Museum.

22 Embroidered casket, 1671. Martha Edlin embroidered this when she was 11 years old. The panels may have been supplied to her ready-drawn and sent to a casket maker to be assembled after she had embroidered them. Wood covered in panels of satin, embroidered with coloured silks and metal thread. [h. 24.5cm]. VAM T.432-1990

23 Sampler, 1668. This is the earliest surviving piece of needlework from a group by Martha Edlin, the daughter of a landowning family, completed when she was eight years old. It was normal for young women in prosperous families to learn needlework in the 17th century. Samplers were made to show the development of their skills through a range of stitches and techniques. Linen embroidered in silks. VAM T.433-1990.

24 A page of patterns for embroidery motifs, 1632. Plate from Richard Shorleyker's *A Scholehouse for the Needle*, 1632. This plate shows patterns for the isolated naturalistic motifs that were a characteristically English form of embroidery. Initially they were based on illustrations in herbals, but by the early 17th century patterns were being supplied by print sellers specifically for the use of embroiderers. VAM 95.O.50.

4. New materials and new techniques

A steady stream of decorative artefacts made from new materials and employing new manufacturing techniques flowed into Tudor and Stuart Britain. One current in this flow was the arrival of previously unknown or unfamiliar materials and techniques from the world beyond Europe – porcelain from China, lacquer from Japan, cotton chintz from India, carpets from Turkey, dyestuffs like cochineal and logwood from the Americas. A second current was import substitution, by which the British learned to make previously unattainable decorative goods. These were predominantly goods originally supplied from continental Europe: the tapestries, swords, firearms, brasswares, woollens, linens, silks, glass, ceramics and myriad other items

25

25 Goblet and cover, about 1695. Made in England. This tall goblet was probably intended for ceremonial or communal drinking. Lead glass. [h. 36cm]. VAM C.536-1936.

that were so frequently listed by Tudor statesmen exasperated at England's dependence on foreigners. A third current – the least powerful one, but nevertheless an important precursor of developments in the eighteenth and nineteenth centuries – was the development in Britain of new materials like lead glass and of new techniques like William Lee's knitting machine.

Of course import substitution was not confined to goods previously made in Europe. The British tried to mimic almost all the new manufactured goods from the industrially advanced areas of Asia. In some cases, most notably in the making of porcelain, they failed. Even a talented chemist like John Dwight, who in the second half of the seventeenth century successfully mastered the German techniques for making stoneware ceramics, proved unequal to the task. It was only in the mid-eighteenth century that the British began to make porcelain. However, in the case of many other Asian manufactures, like lacquer and carpets, the British succeeded before the end of the seventeenth century in producing imitations that could sell, at least in the home market. The history of Indian cotton chintzes in Britain illustrates the whole sequence, from early imports to British manufacture.

26

27

26 Japanned chair, about 1700. Made in England. It has a curving back splat and cabriole legs, a new style that may have been influenced by Chinese furniture. It is painted or japanned in imitation of red Chinese lacquer. Beech wood japanned in gold and green on a red ground; modern upholstery. VAM W.44-1938.

27 Japanese box, about 1600. Wood covered in black lacquer, with gold hiramaki-e lacquer and shell. VAM W.450-1922.

GOODS FROM THE INDIES

Dinah Winch

In Tudor and Stuart Britain much of Asia and the Americas was known indiscriminately as 'The Indies'. The use of the term was not simply a matter of poor geographical knowledge. It reflected how the different parts of the globe that were opened up to direct European trade from the late fifteenth century came to be endowed with a shared exotic allure. This was particularly evident in the great demand for goods brought from 'The Indies' to Europe. Decorative items and curiosities from Asia – primarily India, China and Japan – had long been a by-product of the lucrative trade in spices. However, after the founding of the Dutch and English East India Companies at the start of the seventeenth century, the expansion of trade and cultural exchange began to have a significant effect on the design of goods produced in both Britain and 'The Indies'.

Goods that had once been cabinet pieces, above all porcelain, became common enough to be in daily use in wealthy households. Asian producers of luxury commodities developed export styles to cater for the expanding European market. The decoration of Japanese export lacquer was self-consciously exotic, in contrast to the sparser aesthetic of goods produced for the domestic Japanese market. Similarly, Indian producers adapted both Indian and European designs on printed cottons to suit European tastes. The flowering tree design, which was an amalgam of Asian and European patterns, featured on both Indian and British textiles. The success of Asian artefacts stimulated British production of

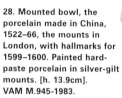

28. Mounted bowl, the porcelain made in China, 1522–66, the mounts in London, with hallmarks for 1599–1600. Painted hard-paste porcelain in silver-gilt mounts. [h. 13.9cm]. VAM M.945-1983.

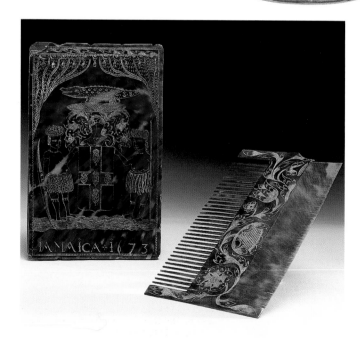

29. Comb case and comb, 1673. Made in Jamaica. Carved and engraved tortoiseshell. [h. 19.5cm]. VAM 524-1877.

30. Panel for a room, about 1696. By Robert Robinson. Oil on wood. VAM P.6-1954.

31. Teapot, the form based on a Chinese porcelain wine pot, about 1685. Marked 'RH'. One of the earliest surviving English teapots. Silver-gilt. [h. 14.6cm]. VAM M.48-1939.

32. Coffee pot imitating a Turkish form, with London hallmarks for 1681–2. Maker's mark of 'GG', probably for George Garthorne. Given by Richard Sterne to the Honourable East India Company. The earliest known English silver coffee pot. Silver, with leather-covered handle. [h. 25cm]. VAM M.398-1921.

34. Detail of a bed curtain, 1690–1710. Made in England. The pattern influenced by Indian painted textiles. Linen and cotton twill, embroidered with wool. VAM 72C-1897.

imitations, such as japanned wares and delftware. These were given the necessary exotic appeal by simulating Asian manufacturing processes (as in the case of japanning) and by combining colours and motifs in ways that appeared Asian to European eyes. The new beverages of tea and coffee adapted vessel forms from the countries in which they originated.

While Europeans did not import decorative goods from the Americas in anything like the quantity they brought from Asia, the Americas did have an impact on British decorative arts.

They were an increasingly important source of commodities such as silver, gold, precious stones, hardwoods and dyes. The imagery of the American goods and peoples had a significant effect on British design as it became incorporated into the multi-layered imagery of the non-European world. The fusion of the fantastic East and West is often lavishly illustrated in early chinoiserie decoration. In the late seventeenth century whole decorative schemes employing such imagery were devised as showcases for imported objects such as porcelain and lacquer.

33. Cabinet, about 1700. Made in England imitating Japanese examples built for export. Japanned wood. VAM W.9:1-1936.

35. Detail of a hanging, about 1700. Made in western India for the European market. Painted and dyed cotton (chintz). VAM IS.156-1953.

The principal objectives of the founders of the English East India Company in 1600 were to sell English woollens in Asia and to secure a direct supply of spices from south-east Asia. For centuries India had been renowned for the supply of cotton textiles with fast and brilliant dye-colours to the lands around the Indian Ocean, but in its early years the East India Company imported few Indian textiles for use in England. Those few were luxury items, such as quilts and hangings, that sold or were given away as curiosities. Gradually the company began to develop a market in England for fine Indian decorated cottons for use as table and bed linens, wall hangings and other household furnishings, but the quantity imported remained small before 1660. One of the key limitations here was their design. Before the middle of the seventeenth century the company's agents in India bought cottons that had been painted, printed or embroidered according to the requirements of Indian and other Asian consumers. Such designs had only a limited appeal in England.

37

The crucial innovation came in 1643, when the company began to require its agents in India to insist that the designs on the cloth be changed to accord with English taste. Those quilts 'which hereafter you shall send we desire may be with more white ground, and the flowers and branch to be in colours in the middle of the quilt as the painter pleases, whereas now most part of your quilts come with sad red grounds which are not so well accepted here'. In other words, the Indian preference for a pattern against a coloured ground was now reversed in favour of the European taste for a pattern in silhouette against a white ground. In the 1660s the company went one step further and began to send sample patterns for chintz, quilts and hangings for the Indian workers to copy. The result was the use of two-dimensional forms and motifs that were perceived in England as Indian, but which in fact came to India from England. The late seventeenth-century Indian chintzes that became so popular for women's garments may have retained an exotic allure for their English wearers, but the range of patterns and motifs they employed often had more to do with English constructions of the exotic than with Indian visual culture.

36

36 Long cushion cover, first quarter of the 17th century. A piece of English embroidery employing some of the chinoiserie motifs usually associated with the Tree of Life designs found on 17th-century Indian cottons. It predates most imported Indian cottons, however, suggesting that the source for such designs was English. Linen canvas embroidered with silk; wool and metal thread mainly in tent stitch. [l. 100cm]. VAM 816-1893.

37 Painted cotton coverlet, mid-17th century. Made in the Deccan, western India, for the Indian market. It has a red ground of the sort that the East India Company rejected for export to Europe. Painted and dyed cotton. [l. 89.5cm]. VAM IS.34-1969.

38

The design of these two hangings, one made in India and the other in England, derives from the same source. They are not identical. One is the reverse of the other and they differ in a number of minor respects. Nevertheless, they are both clearly adaptations of a single original design, probably taken from a pattern book of the kind published in 17th-century England for the use of embroiderers. It was patterns of this kind that the East India Company sent to India from the 1660s to be used in the manufacture of decorated cotton cloth for sale in England (*see also 5:34 and 35*).

39

38 Detail of a bed or wall hanging, about 1700. Made in Gujarat, western India, for the English market. Cotton embroidered with silk; chain stitch. VAM IS.155-1953.

39 Detail of a crewelwork bed hanging, about 1680. Embroidered in England. Linen and cotton embroidered with wool. © 2003 Museum of Fine Arts, Boston.

40

41

42

This reworking of designs was necessary because the East India Company was entering a market in which it faced stiff competition from a variety of new European decorated cloths, including woven silks and the light worsted cloths known in England as the 'new draperies', as well as from various styles of embroidery. Indeed, sixteenth- and seventeenth-century Europe witnessed a tide of innovation in decorated fabrics of many kinds.

In the face of this competition, the East India Company's policy of dictating design from London was enormously successful. By the 1680s its imports from India were running at more than one million pieces of cloth a year, many of them decorated fabrics intended for furnishing or clothing. This rising tide of imports was the cause of much resentment in England. One response was to imitate Indian fast colour techniques on cotton or linen cloth. From the 1670s copies were manufactured in London, using block printing in preference to the labour-intensive process of painting predominant in India. By the early years of the eighteenth century the East India Company was complaining that printing could be done in England at half the price charged for Indian goods and in better colours and patterns. A second response was the campaign by British manufacturers of silks and light worsted cloths (themselves both import substitutes) to have all dyed or decorated cottons, whether imported from India or not, banned outright. The campaign culminated in 1721 in a legal prohibition that was to last 50 years.

---

40 Detail of a woven silk, third quarter of the 17th century. Probably woven in England. VAM T.14-1922.

41 Detail of a striped worsted, early 18th century. Woven at Norwich or Spitalfields, London. Part of a Portuguese chasuble. Portugal was an important export market for English worsteds. Combed wool, woven. VAM T.287-1962.

42 Printed cotton 'calico', 1690–1700. Made in England or the Netherlands. The scale of its design suggests that it was intended for bed hangings. Cotton, block-printed. VAM 12-1884.

Like cotton printing, the history of the making of fine, decorative glass in Tudor and Stuart Britain began with imports and attempts to copy them. Unlike cotton printing, it culminated in radical innovations in the kind of material used and in the appearance of the objects made from it. In part these innovations were the result of British inventiveness. In the sixteenth century the British, like most Europeans, imported drinking glasses from Venice made of the clear cristallo glass for which that city was renowned. British-made glass was crude, green and opaque. Italians introduced the manufacture of crystal glass to Antwerp early in the century and in 1567 a Protestant refugee glass maker from Antwerp, Jean Carré, arrived in England, at roughly the same time as many other skilled Antwerp craftspeople escaping religious persecution, including various silk and woollen weavers. Within a year Carré had started manufacturing crystal glass in the Venetian manner at Crutched Friars in London. Subsequently he imported nine Venetian glass workers, one of whom, Jacomo Verzelini, took over the business. In 1574 Verzelini was granted a 21-year monopoly to make drinking glasses of the Venetian type, protected by a ban on Venetian imports.

With the aid of its monopoly, the business prospered. By the early seventeenth century, after Verzelini's retirement, it was managed by an English glass maker, William Robson, suggesting that the Venetians' skills had been successfully transferred to native workers. By 1620 the Venetian ambassador was complaining that English crystal glass rivalled the Venetian product in quality, although large quantities of Venetian glass were also being imported: more than 10,000 glasses in 1626. It was at this period that the first major British technical innovation occurred – the introduction of coal fuel. Previously glass had been made using wood to heat the raw materials to the very high temperatures required, but in the early seventeenth century a method was developed of preventing the molten glass coming into contact with the fuel, using closed clay pots. This allowed coal, which was abundant in Britain, to be used to fuel the glass furnaces, in spite of its noxious impurities. The subsequent shift of the whole industry to coal firing was exceptionally rapid, because in 1615 the government, desperate for revenue, transferred the monopoly of glass making to the promoters of the new process and banned the use of other fuels. It is important to stress, however, that this change would almost certainly have happened eventually without government intervention. One of the most significant technological developments in Stuart Britain was the shift to coal and coke firing for the smelting and refining of copper, lead, brass and a host of other materials used in the high-design trades.

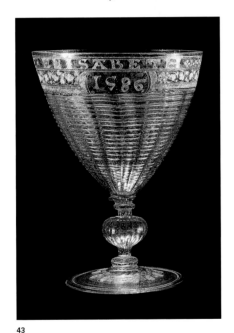

43

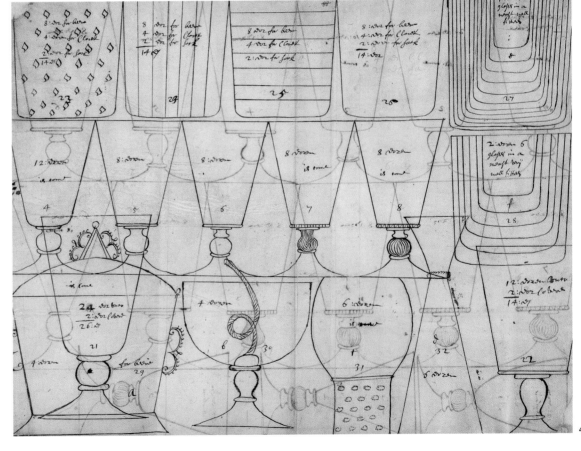

44

43 Goblet, 1586. Made in London by Jacomo Verzelini. Engraved by Anthony de Lysle. Glass with mould-blown stem, gilt, trailed decoration and diamond-point engraving. VAM C.226-1983.

44 Page of a manuscript containing letters and drawings of glass designs, sent by John Greene of London to his Venetian agent Alessio Morelli, 17 September 1669. The drawings are specifications for the drinking glasses that Greene was ordering from Venice. Ink and paper. The British Library.

The new fuel contributed to the success of two significant innovations in objects made from glass. The British made a major contribution to each of them. The first was the development of the glass wine bottle, the result of the discovery that if the pots used to hold the molten glass were left uncovered in the coal-fired furnaces, a dark, almost black glass resulted that excluded light and was ideal for storing wine. The second was lead glass. In 1674 George Ravenscroft, a wealthy English merchant in the Venetian trade who had set up a glass house in the Savoy area in London, sought a patent for a process to make 'a particular sort of Christaline Glasse resembling Rock Cristall'. Ravenscroft's glass was distinctive because it contained large quantities of lead oxide. The use of lead in glass was not new – the Venetians were familiar with its use in the manufacture of paste jewels, and all over Europe glassmakers in the mid-seventeenth century were looking for ways to make a heavier, more sturdy glass. But Ravenscroft helped perfect and market the new kind of glass, drawing on techniques introduced shortly before in the Netherlands. The new technique spread widely in British glass-houses even before Ravenscroft's patent expired in 1681. Lead glass was heavy, slow-cooling and impossible to blow thinly or to ornament with fine pulled threads. It resulted in a style of drinking glass and other vessels with bold, simple forms and little decoration that came to be seen as distinctively British, although a British preference for simplicity was already apparent in the glass the Venetians were supplying to London before Ravenscroft's innovation.

46

45

45 Wine bottles, 1660–1720. Made in England.
Right: free-blown glass, 1660–70. Centre: free-blown glass, stamped with a dated seal, 1693. Left: blown and rolled glass, stamped with a dated seal, 1720.
VAM C.382-1993, C.383-1993, C.113-1945.

46 Wine glass, 1700–10. Made in England. Lead glass with baluster stem.
VAM C.233-1912.

5. New products

Innovation in the Tudor and Stuart period was not just a matter of new techniques and materials. Britain also saw the appearance of an astonishing number of artefacts that were new in kind, irrespective of how they were made or what they were made from. They included punch bowls and wallpaper, upholstered chairs and longcase clocks, bookcases and snuff boxes. Some, like the clay tobacco pipe, were among the many new products that emerged as a result of Britain's engagement with the world beyond Europe. Some, like the newspaper, took advantage of the opportunity to sell information offered by the new technologies of printing and paper making. Others, like the 30-piece silver toilet services given to many noblewomen on marriage, reflected the way that apparently intimate activities like getting dressed became occasions for spectacular display in grand seventeenth-century houses. But there was more to the novelty of these objects than just the circumstances that called them into being. They challenged previous assumptions about product identity – about *how* things were to be used and how one object might differ from another.

47 Bookcase, about 1695. Probably made by a London joiner. From the library at Dyrham Park, Gloucestershire, the house of William Blathwayt. Oak, crown glass and iron. VAM W.12-1927.

48 Wallpaper, about 1550–75. From Besford Court, Worcestershire. Made in England. Printed with woodblocks. VAM E.3593-1913.

THE BOOK

Rowan Watson

Printing with movable type was invented by the German goldsmith, Johann Gutenberg, at Mainz in Germany in the 1450s. William Caxton probably encountered the new technology when on business in Germany and Flanders; he imported it to London in 1476. Nonetheless, Britain continued to rely heavily on books published abroad. Until the Protestant Reformation in the 1530s, books for personal devotions (especially Books of Hours) were mostly imported. In terms of design, continental printing set standards that English printers emulated.

The works of Caxton and his successors employed the same letter shapes and page design as handwritten books, but most English ornament and illustration appeared crude when compared to continental products. Gothic types were widely used – popular works such as almanacs were printed with them until after the seventeenth century. Roman type, which was first used in England in 1508, and italic fonts became more common after the mid-sixteenth century.

49. *The Golden Legend*, 1527. By Jacobus de Voragine; translated by William Caxton. Printed in London by Wynkyn de Worde. Illustrated with woodcuts. VAM 86.F.93.

50. *The first tome or volume of the Paraphrases of Erasmus upon the Newe Testament*, 1551. By Desiderius Erasmus. Published in London by Edward Whitechurche. VAM 86.F.91.

The use of avant-garde Renaissance ornament in books became increasingly common as the sixteenth century progressed, through the use of woodcuts, but books relating to religious matters reflected the Anglican preference after the 1530s for the word and text, rather than the image. Nevertheless, the official Bible of 1539 had a carefully composed frontispiece that demonstrated pictorially Henry VIII's position as head of the Church and, for some works, images remained essential. John Foxe's *Book of Martyrs* (first edition 1563) needed images for accounts of Protestants who had died for their faith. Puritans were, however, on the whole hostile to images for religious works. In 1640 Archbishop Laud was attacked for sanctioning the publication of bibles with images, although prints to stick into bibles were available for those of the high-church persuasion.

Illustrations printed with engraved metal plates (often engraved in the Low Countries) began to be used in books in the latter part of the sixteenth century, although engraved title-pages replete with allegorical and emblematic allusions, usually arranged around a Roman arch, only became common after 1600. The superior quality of engraved images ensured that they were widely used in the seventeenth century: maps, scientific and antiquarian books and manuals of all kinds could now be systematically illustrated to unprecedented levels of quality.

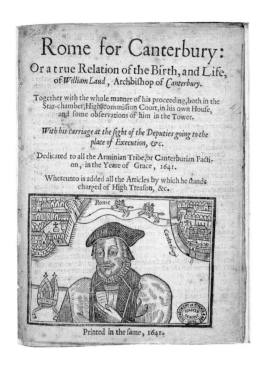

51. The pamphlet *Rome for Canterbury: or a . . . life, of William Laud*, 1641. VAM Forster:5177.

52. *Paradise Lost. A poem in twelve books*, 4th edition, 1688. By John Milton. Illustrations engraved by Michael Burgesse after designs by John Baptist Medina. Printed in London by Miles Flesher. Published by Richard Bentley and Jacob Tonson. VAM Dyce:6606.

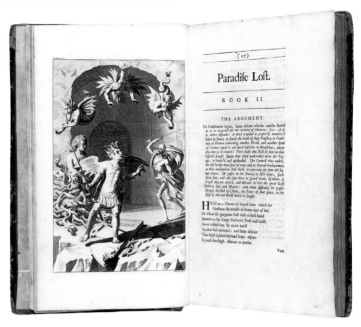

From the 1620s entrepreneurial publishers such as John Wright specialized in cheap ballads, news pamphlets, plays and 'penny books'; by 1700 the chapbook, often illustrated with a woodcut, was delivered around the kingdom by pedlars and travelling salesmen, who supplemented a distributive network established by publishers and booksellers.

53. Title-page and frontispiece of *An epicede or funerall song on the most disastrous death of . . . Henry Prince of Wales*, 1612. By George Chapman. Printed in London by Thomas Snodham. Published by John Budge, London. Letter-press, with an engraving by William Hole. VAM Dyce:2040.

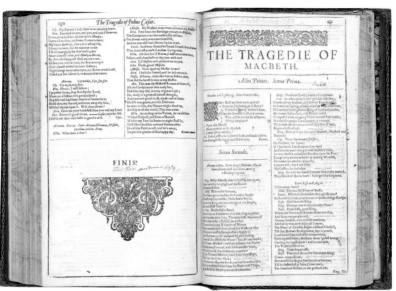

54. *Mr William Shakespeares comedies, histories & tragedies. Published according to the true originall copies*, 1623 (The 'First Folio'). By William Shakespeare. Printed in London by Isaac Jaggard and Edward Blount. VAM Forster:7884.

55. *The second volume of the ecclesiastical history contaynyng the Actes and monumentes*, 1596, popularly known as *Foxe's Book of Martyrs*. By John Foxe. Printed in London by Peter Short, assignee of Richard Day. Illustrated with woodcuts. VAM 86.G.55.

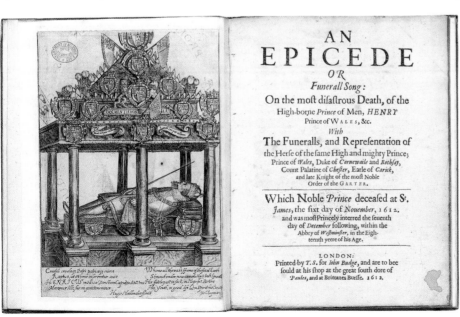

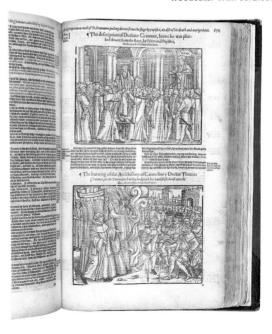

56

57

56 The Calverley toilet service, with London hallmarks for 1683–4. Maker's mark of William Fowle. The reliefs on the lids cast from plaquettes by Guglielmo della Porta. The service consists of one mirror frame, two tazzas, two large round boxes with lids and two small round boxes with lids, two rectangular boxes with lids, two large vessels with lids and two small vases with lids, and one pincushion. Silver, cast and chased. VAM 240-1879.

57 Detail of the front page of *The Post Man* newspaper, no. 1024, 3–6 October 1702. Printed in London. Letter-press and woodcut. The British Library.

Numb. 1024 CCCC

The Post Man:

And the Historical Account, &c.

From **Saturday** October 3, to **Tuesday** October 6, 1702.

Milan, Sept. 27.

ON *Sunday* last, being the anniversary of the Birth of the Queen of *Spain*, the Princess of *Vaudemont* gave a noble entertainment to the Persons of the chief Quality of both Sexes. Letters from the Camp near *Luzara* say, that the King of *Spain* in-

a readiness to fall upon their Rear if possible, for tho we are incamped within a Musket shot of their Works, yet the Country is so difficult, by reason of Canals, Ditches and little Brooks, that 'tis very likely they will decamp without any Action. Our Parties obtain frequent advantages over them, and have brought several Prisoners since our last. One of them seized 3 days ago 7 large Boats going down the Po, to be imployed for the Bridge near *Gonfula*; they killed 7 French men therein, and brought away a Wars

Tobacco pipes were disposable, rarely being reused more than three or four times, and had constantly to be replaced. So too did the newspaper, but its disposability arose from the fact that old news would not sell. It was one of a number of seventeenth-century innovations that traded on built-in obsolescence. Like the introduction of seasonal changes in the design of fashionable silk fabrics, the newspaper intensified the distinction between the old and the new, accelerating the commercial cycle and organizing it on a regular basis, weekly or even daily. But this was not the only tactic for ensuring sales by manipulating product identity. The silver toilet service represented another tactic, binding the customer to a single supplier by providing objects in standardized sets that matched in terms of material, form and decoration.

These new kinds of ephemerality and standardization demonstrate how the ever-growing variety of artefacts in circulation pushed Tudor and Stuart manufacturers towards new ways of making their products distinctive. The pressures on them could be considerable. An innovation made from one material might threaten the livelihoods of producers in other materials. Yet, at the same time, it might provide inventive manufacturers in those materials with an opportunity to extend their range.

One of the most striking instances of this process is the development of the silver teapot in London between 1660 and 1714. As tea slowly became an established commodity in Britain from the 1660s, it was made mainly in ceramic teapots and wine pots that were imported from China. Asian porcelain pots were imitated in tin-glazed earthenware by London delftware potters, and red stoneware teapots from Yixing in China were imitated by John Dwight at Fulham and by the Elers brothers at their factories at Vauxhall and in Staffordshire. But at roughly the same time as these English imitations were being undertaken in ceramic materials, there occurred a much more radical reformulation of the Chinese teapot form as a silver object, which had no immediate direct precedents either in China or in England.

58 Tobacco pipe, 17th century. Made in England. Pipe clay. The Museum of London.

59 Chinese pear-shaped stoneware teapot, 1650–60. Red stoneware teapots of this kind were produced at Yixing in China and imported to Europe by the Dutch during the 17th century. Unglazed red stoneware. [h. 7.5cm]. VAM C.871-1936.

60 Teapot imitating Chinese stoneware teapots, 1690–8. Made by David and John Philip Elers at Bradwell Wood, Staffordshire. Slip-cast, unglazed red stoneware with moulded panels and unfired gilding. [h. 8.9cm]. VAM C.4-1932.

As has often subsequently been the case with new artefacts, there was initially a marked indeterminacy about the form of these new silver teapots. It was not until the start of the eighteenth century that some degree of design stability was achieved as a limited range of type forms became dominant. The first surviving English silver teapot was presented to the directors of the East India Company in 1670 by George, Lord Berkeley. Its shape had no obvious Chinese or Japanese parallels and it was much larger than most East Asian teapots (which were mostly less than 15cm in height). However, it closely resembled the typical coffee pot used in London coffee houses of the period. At this date, although both tea and coffee were recent novelties, coffee drinking had become much better established. In coffee houses, large pots with lids in the Turkish style, like the lid of the East India Company teapot, were used for serving numerous customers.

Other silver teapots made in London in the 1660s and 1670s were much smaller. None survive, but they probably resembled the pear-shaped silver teapots of the 1680s, which weighed under 285g, were less than 15cm tall and loosely followed the forms of Chinese

63

ceramic tea and wine pots (see 5:31). By the first two decades of the eighteenth century, when tea consumption began to increase rapidly, silver teapot design had stabilized around this smaller size of pot, with two forms dominant – the plain, squat, pear shape and the globular, 'bullet' shape. Both survive in smooth and polygonal versions; both derived from Chinese ceramic forms, although the techniques of manufacture and the overall visual effect were radically different from Chinese teapots. They were much more suited than the East India Company teapot for making tea in limited quantities, for drinking by individuals or small groups, and they were immensely successful.

62

64

61 Still life with Chinese blue-and-white porcelain teapot, silver jar and candlestick, about 1695. Probably painted in London, by an unknown artist. Oil on canvas. VAM P.2-1939.

62 An English pear-shaped teapot, with London hallmarks for 1713–14. Maker's mark of Thomas Folkingham. Silver, with replacement wooden handle. [h. 14cm]. VAM M.224-1930.

63 Detail of a tile panel showing a coffee-house boy with a coffee pot, late 17th century. Tin-glazed earthenware. The Museum of London.

64 The first surviving English silver teapot, with London hallmarks for 1670–1. Maker's mark of TL. Engraved with the arms of the East India Company and of Lord Berkeley. Silver, engraved; handle of leather and wood. [h. 35cm]. VAM M.399-1921.

SILVERWARES

Helen Clifford

Between 1500 and 1714 developments in silverware were driven more by social and political changes at home, and new ideas from continental Europe, than by technical innovation. The greatest single influence was the Protestant Reformation. It witnessed a change in the character of church plate, from the smaller Catholic chalice to the larger Protestant communion cup, and was accompanied by a demand for secular plate, buoyed by economic prosperity among the élite. As a result there was an increase not only in the number of dining, drinking and dressing wares being made, but also in their variety.

Increased demand stimulated the appearance of novel kinds of objects, such as tankards, casting bottles and spice plates. Older forms, like the standing salt, were replaced by smaller, cheaper designs, like the bell salt, which appears in inventories from the 1530s. Their manufacture (comprising two tapering sections) required no great technical ability, and they could easily be chased and engraved with the latest Renaissance strapwork ornament. Most of the new forms were based on French and Dutch models, although the steeple cup, which appears in royal plate inventories from the 1570s, was peculiarly English and was intended to enhance the splendour of the buffet display. Some continental habits, like the use of the fork – common in court circles in Italy in the 1530s – took longer to arrive in England. The earliest-known English example, a silver fork of 1632, is based on a continental design source.

67. Bell salt, with London hallmarks for 1594–5. Marked 'NR' conjoined over four pellets in a plain shield. Chased silver-gilt. VAM 283:1&2-1893.

The design and decoration of English silver were generally unadventurous. The main exception was an early flickering of the Dutch auricular style. It first reached England just before the civil war, although it did not become more widespread until the Restoration of Charles II in 1660. The muscular dissolving borders of the silver-gilt porringer of about 1665 are a high-quality example of the style. The Restoration coincided with the spread of new French modes of dining, which required refinements in silver tableware. It also saw the introduction of silver serving equipment for new beverages, such as tea, coffee, chocolate and punch. It was at this period, too, that silver objects began to proliferate in the bedroom, with the introduction of toilet services. The arrival of large numbers of skilled French Protestant goldsmiths – the Huguenots – after 1685 helped the goldsmiths' trade in England satisfy the demand for the new objects, since they brought with them innovatory forms, like the helmet-shaped ewer, and decorative techniques, like cut-card work.

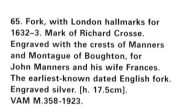

65. Fork, with London hallmarks for 1632–3. Mark of Richard Crosse. Engraved with the crests of Manners and Montague of Boughton, for John Manners and his wife Frances. The earliest-known dated English fork. Engraved silver. [h. 17.5cm]. VAM M.358-1923.

66. Communion cup and cover, about 1571–4. Mark of John Jones of Exeter. Silver, with gilded interior, die-struck and punched foot-rings and wires on base; engraving on band around cup and on cover. VAM 4636-1858.

68. Font cup, with London hallmarks for 1500–1. Mark of a device in a shaped shield; originally the property of the Campion family of Danny, Sussex. Silver-gilt. VAM M.249-1924.

71. Porringer, about 1665. Mark of a star above an escallop with six pellets. Engraved with the arms of Anthony Ashley Cooper, later Earl of Shaftesbury. Embossed and chased silver-gilt. VAM M.104-1984.

70. Steeple cup, with London hallmarks for 1625–6. Marked 'TF', possibly the mark of Thomas Flynt. Given by Richard Chester to the Corporation of Trinity House in 1632. Chased and embossed silver-gilt. VAM M.244-1924.

69. Helmet-shaped ewer, with London hallmarks for 1700–1. Mark of David Willaume. Engraved with arms of the diplomat and public servant, the Honourable and Reverend Richard Hill of Hawkestone, Shropshire. Silver-gilt with cast details and applied cut-card work, ornamented in relief. VAM 822-1890.

72. Silver wire-work purse, 1630–50. Silver-gilt filigree with silk lining and tassels. VAM M.17-1989.

73 *Sovereign of the Seas*, 1637. By John
Payne. Hand-coloured engraving. © National
Maritime Museum, London.

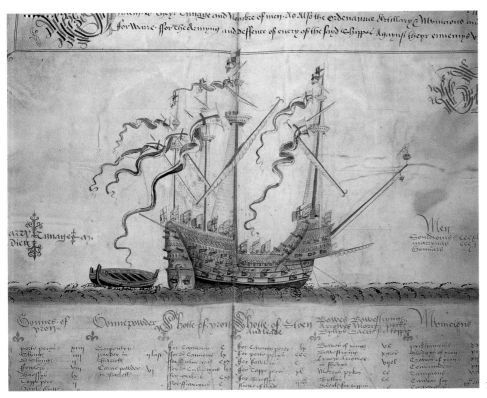

74

75

The development of the silver teapot was a response to the new and competitive market for hot-drink utensils, but not all competition in Tudor and Stuart Britain was commercial. Another new British artefact of the seventeenth century – the three-deck warship – is testimony to competitiveness of a very different sort: the military and propaganda struggle between European states. The *Sovereign of the Seas*, completed in 1637 for Charles I, was the first great warship to be built with three gun decks. Charles's predecessors had also built great ships, like Henry VIII's *Henri Grâce à Dieu* and James I and VI's *Prince Royal*. Often considerations of royal prestige had been as influential as strict naval necessity. Prestige certainly loomed large when Charles I informed the leading English shipbuilder, Phineas Pett, of his 'princely resolution for the building of a great new ship'. The *Sovereign of the Seas* was designed to impress. She was huge and, in contrast to the *Prince Royal* of 1610, also designed by Pett, she was a genuine three-decker. She carried a massive armament of 102 guns, almost twice the earlier ship's 55, and outgunned her Dutch and French rivals.

Built at a cost of £65,587, the *Sovereign of the Seas* was extraordinarily expensive, ten times the price of the average 40- to 50-gun warship. Part of this expense arose from the cost of the ship's decoration. Great naval vessels in the seventeenth century were always highly decorated, especially at the bow and stern, but the decorative work on the *Sovereign of the Seas* was exceptional, costing £6,691 alone, executed by the carvers John and Mathias Christmas.

Her figurehead was King Edgar the Peaceful on horseback; her stern carried figures of Victory, Neptune, Jason, Jupiter and Hercules. In service, much of this decoration had to be removed to improve her stability, but its cost and elaboration confirmed the importance that Charles I ascribed to the arts in projecting the dignity and majesty of his kingship in all its aspects. Like the tapestries made at Mortlake or Van Dyck's royal portraits, the *Sovereign of the Seas* was an exercise in the aesthetics of royal power.

Critics among shipbuilders warned that 'the art or wit of man cannot build a ship fit for service with three tier of ordnance', but their views dissuaded neither the King nor Pett, a designer who in some respects stood outside the dominant tradition of the craftsman-shipwright. The result was a vessel that was far less manoeuvrable than most of her predecessors and one that concentrated a much greater proportion of her firepower in the broadside, rather than fore and aft. In the sixteenth century, when naval tactics emphasized turning and boarding, these characteristics would have been a disadvantage. But in the Anglo-Dutch War of 1652–4 the British developed the devastating new tactic of fighting in a single line of battle, in which each ship had to hold its position. *Sovereign of the Seas* was well suited to this, and she became the vessel that set the pattern for the three-deckers built in large numbers in the second half of the seventeenth century. Ships of this configuration were to remain the most powerful naval vessels and, indeed, the largest ships in the world, until steam replaced sail in the nineteenth century.

74 *Henri Grâce à Dieu*, 1545–6. Detail from the Anthony Anthony Roll. Built for Henry VIII in 1514, she was rebuilt between 1536 and 1539. Watercolour on vellum. Pepys Library, Magdalene College, Cambridge.

75 Medal, 1639. Cast in London by the Frenchman Nicolas Briot. Charles I issued medals to promote his royal authority and to publicize his policies, including his maritime ambitions. This medal, depicting on its reverse a naval vessel in full sail, asserted his sovereign authority over the English Channel. The inscription reads NEC META MIHI QVAE TERMINVS ORBI (Nor to me is that a limit, which is boundary to the world). Cast silver. VAM 949-1901.

The pattern of innovation in design and the decorative arts experienced in Tudor and Stuart Britain, combining imports from abroad with native inventiveness, was not new. Innovations in the material culture of Venice and Florence in the fifteenth century, or Antwerp and Paris in the sixteenth, derived from a similar combination of external and internal sources. Britain was a latecomer, often soaking up new influences from southern Europe and Asia at second or third hand. But in the seventeenth century, especially, her location on Europe's favoured north-west seaboard, her aggressive trading policy and her resources (both human and natural) worked to produce an immensely successful commercial economy. In this fertile soil it was possible for the manufacture of high-design goods, previously lacking in sophistication, to approach the highest western European standards of aesthetics and technique. Nevertheless, it was only to be in the course of the century after 1714 – the year when the last Stuart monarch, Queen Anne, died – that Britain came to share in setting those standards.

76 *Peter Pett and the Sovereign of the Seas,* about 1660. By Sir Peter Lely. The painting shows the elaborately carved stern of the ship after rebuilding in 1660, when she was renamed the *Royal Sovereign*. The shipwright Peter Pett, the builder of *Sovereign of the Seas*, was the son of the ship's designer, Phineas Pett. Oil on canvas. © National Maritime Museum, London.

Chronology of Events and Publications, 1485–1714

DATES	POLITICAL EVENTS	DESIGN, ART AND SCIENCE	PUBLICATIONS
1485	Death of Richard III of England, accession of Henry VII		
1492	Christopher Columbus sails to the Americas from Spain		
1498	Vasco da Gama sails to India from Portugal		
1503		Building of Henry VII's chapel at Westminster Abbey begins	
1509	Death of Henry VII of England, accession of Henry VIII		
1511–18	England at war with France		
1513	Death of James IV of Scotland at the Battle of Flodden Field, accession of James V		
1515		King's College chapel, Cambridge, completed	
1517	Martin Luther initiates the Reformation in Germany		
1519–22	Ferdinand Magellan's voyage to circumnavigate the world		
1520	Henry VIII meets Francis I of France at the Field of Cloth of Gold, France		
1522–5	England at war with France		
1533	Henry VIII divorces Catherine of Aragon		
1534	Act of Supremacy ends papal jurisdiction in England		
1535			Miles Coverdale's English translation of the Bible
1536	Union of Wales with England Dissolution of the monasteries		
1542	Death of James V of Scotland, accession of Mary, Queen of Scots		
1543–6	England at war with France		
1547	Death of Henry VIII of England, accession of Edward VI	Building of Somerset House, London, begins	
1548			Thomas Geminus, *Morysse and Damashin renewed and encreased Very profitable for Goldsmythes and Embroiderars*
1549			Sir Thomas Smith, *Discourse of this Common Weal of this Realm of England*
1553	Death of Edward VI of England, accession of Mary I		
1553–8	Roman Catholicism re-established in England		
1557–9	England at war with France		
1557	Loss of Calais		
1558	Death of Mary I of England, accession of Elizabeth I		
1560s	Persecution of Protestants in the Low Countries results in large-scale emigration		
1560	Scottish Parliament abolishes papal jurisdiction and the mass		
1563			John Foxe, *Actes and Monuments* (or *Book of Martyrs*) John Shute, *The First and Chief Groundes of Architecture*
1566		Building of the Royal Exchange, London, begins	
1567		Building of Longleat House, Wiltshire, begins Venetian glass first made in England	
1568	Mary, Queen of Scots exiled in England, accession of James VI		
1577			Hans Vredeman de Vries, *Architectura* William Harrison, *Description of England*
1580s		William Lee invents the knitting frame	
1585–1604	England at war with Spain		
1587	Execution by the English of Mary, Queen of Scots		
1588	Spanish Armada		
1591		Staging of the first of William Shakespeare's plays Building of Hardwick Hall, Derbyshire, begins	
1594–1603	Nine years war in Ireland		
1599		Globe Theatre built in London	
1600	English East India Company founded		
1603	Death of Elizabeth I of England, accession of James VI of Scotland as James I of England and Ireland		
1607	First permanent English settlement in the Americas at Jamestown, Virginia		
1609		The New Exchange, London, opened	
1611			Authorized version of the Bible English translation of Sebastiano Serlio, *The First Booke of Architecture*

DATES	POLITICAL EVENTS	DESIGN, ART AND SCIENCE	PUBLICATIONS
1612		Coal first used to make glass	
1616		Building of Queen's House, Greenwich, begins	
1619		Building of Banqueting House, Whitehall, begins	
		Mortlake tapestry works established	
1624–30	War with Spain		
1624			Sir Henry Wootton, *Elements of Architecture*
1625	Death of James I and VI, accession of Charles I		
1626–30	War with France		
1627	English settlement of Barbados		
1631		Building of the Piazza at Covent Garden begins	
1632		Anthony Van Dyck settles in England as court painter	
1642–6	English Civil War		
1649	Execution of Charles I		
about 1650		Coal first used to make earthenware	
		Building of Coleshill, Berkshire, begins	
1652–4	First Dutch War		
1655	English capture of Jamaica from Spain		
1657		The first English coffee house opens in Oxford	
1658	Death of Oliver Cromwell, Lord Protector		
1660	Restoration of Charles II	Royal Society established	Samuel Pepys begins his diary
1661	Louis XIV assumes full powers as King of France		Robert Boyle, *The Sceptical Chymist*
1663		Drury Lane Theatre opens in London	
1665–7	Second Dutch War		
1666	Fire of London		
1672		John Dwight establishes his pottery at Fulham	
1672–4	Third Dutch War		
1673		Building of St Paul's Cathedral, London, begins	
1675		Royal Observatory at Greenwich founded	
1678	Popish plot		Joseph Moxon, *Mechanick Exercises*
1679–81	Exclusion crisis		
1680s		Lead, copper and tin first smelted with coal	
1685	Death of Charles II, accession of James II and VII		
	Exodus of Protestant Huguenots from France after Revocation of the Edict of Nantes		
1686		Building of Chatworth House, Derbyshire, begins	
1687			Isaac Newton, *Philosophiae Naturalis Principia Mathematica*
1688	'Glorious Revolution'. Flight of James II and VII		John Stalker and George Parker, *A Treatise of Japanning and Varnishing*
1688–97	Nine Years War		
1689	Accession of William and Mary		
	Bill of Rights		
1690	Toleration Act	Building of Wren's additions to Hampton Court Palace begins	John Locke, *Two Treatises on Government*
1693			Jean Tijou, *A New Book of Drawings, Invented and Designed by Jean Tijou*
1694	Death of Mary II, William III reigns alone		
1695		Lapse of legislation requiring press licensing	
1698		Building of Castle Howard, Yorkshire, begins	
1699		Import of Indian decorated cottons banned	
1701	Act of Settlement		
1702–13	War of Spanish Succession		
1702	Death of William III, accession of Queen Anne		*The Daily Courant*, the first daily newspaper, founded
1707	Act of Union with Scotland	Iron first smelted with coke by Abraham Darby at Coalbrookdale, Shropshire	George Farquhar, *The Beaux' Stratagem*
1709		Copyright Act for books	
1709–11			*The Tatler* magazine published
1711		Sir Godfrey Kneller's drawing academy	Earl of Shaftesbury, *Characteristicks*
1711–12			*The Spectator* magazine published
before 1712		Thomas Newcomen builds his atmospheric steam engine	
1713		East India Company secures right of access to Canton, China	
1714	Death of Queen Anne, accession of George I		Bernard de Mandeville, *The Fable of the Bees*

Design and the Decorative Arts: A Select Bibliography

1. Introduction

Appleby, J. O., *Economic Thought and Ideology in Seventeenth-Century England* (Princeton, NJ, 1978)

Armitage, D., *The Ideolgical Origins of the British Empire* (Cambridge, 2000)

Beier, A. L. and Finlay, R. (eds), *London, 1500–1700: The Making of the Metropolis* (1986)

Berry, C. J., *The Idea of Luxury: a Conceptual and Historical Investigation* (Cambridge, 1994)

Braddick, M. J., *State Formation in Early Modern England, c. 1550–1700* (Cambridge, 2000)

Bradshaw, B. and Morrill, J. (eds), *The British Problem c. 1534–1707: State Formation in the British Archipelago* (1996)

Bryson, A., *From Courtesy to Civility: Changing Codes of Conduct in Early Modern England* (Oxford, 1998)

Canny, N. (ed.), *The Oxford History of the British Empire. Vol. I. Origins of Empire: British Overseas Enterprise to the Close of the Seventeenth Century* (Oxford, 1998)

Clay, C. G. A., *Economic Expansion and Social Change: England 1500–1700* (Cambridge, 1984)

Collinson, P., *The Religion of Protestants: The Church in English Society, 1559–1625* (Oxford, 1982)

Corns, T. N., *The Royal Image: Representations of Charles I* (Cambridge, 1999)

Denvir, B., *From the Middle Ages to the Stuarts. Art, Design and Society before 1689* (1988)

Duffy, E., *The Stripping of the Altars. Traditional Religion in England, 1400–1580* (1992)

Durston, C. and Eales, J. (eds), *The Culture of English Puritanism, 1560–1700* (1996)

Dyer, C., *Standards of Living in the later Middle Ages. Social Change in England c. 1200–1520* (Cambridge, 1989)

Earle, P., *The Making of the English Middle Class: Business, Society and Family Life in London, 1660–1730* (1989)

Ellis, S. G. and Barber, S. (eds), *Conquest and Union: Fashioning a British State, 1485–1625* (1995)

Ford, Boris (ed.), *The Cambridge Guide to the Arts in Britain: Vol. 3. Renaissance and Reformation* (1989)

Ford, Boris (ed.), *The Cambridge Guide to the Arts in Britain: Vol. 4. The Seventeenth Century* (1989)

Gaimster, D. and Stamper, P. (eds), *The Age of Transition: The Archeology of English Culture, 1400–1600* (1997)

Green, I., *Print and Protestantism in Early Modern England* (Cambridge, 2000)

Gwynn, R., *Huguenot Heritage. The History and Contribution of the Huguenots in Britain* (Brighton, 2000)

Haigh, C., *English Reformations: Religion, Politics and Society under the Tudors* (Oxford, 1993)

Harte, N. B., 'State Control of Dress and Social Change in Pre-Industrial England', in Coleman, D. C. and John, A. H. (eds), *Trade, Government and Economy in Pre-Industrial England* (1976)

Hoppit, J., *A Land of Liberty? England, 1689–1727* (Oxford, 2000)

Lubbock, J., *The Tyranny of Taste. The Politics of Architecture and Design in Britain, 1550–1960* (1995)

MacCulloch, D., *The Later Reformation in England, 1574–1603* (1990)

McKellar, E., *The Birth of Modern London. The Development and Design of the City, 1660–1720* (Manchester, 1999)

Milton, A., *Catholic and Reformed. The Roman and Protestant Churches in English Protestant Thought* (Cambridge, 1995)

Morrill, J. (ed.), *The Oxford Illustrated History of Tudor and Stuart Britain* (Oxford, 1996)

Orlin, L. C. (ed.), *Material London, ca. 1600* (Philadelphia, PA, 2000)

Palliser, D. M., *The Age of Elizabeth. England Under the Later Tudors, 1547–1603* (1983)

Pointon, M., 'Quakerism and Visual Culture, 1650–1800', *Art History*, 20 (1997)

Porter, R., *London, A Social History* (1994)

Sekora, J., *Luxury: The Concept in Western Thought, Eden to Smollet* (Baltimore, MD, 1977)

Shammas, C., *The Pre-Industrial Consumer in England and America* (Oxford, 1990)

Sharpe, J., *Early Modern England: A Social History, 1550–1760* (1987)

Sharpe, K. and Lake, P. (eds), *Culture and Politics in Early Stuart England* (1994)

Smout, T. C., *A History of the Scottish People, 1560–1830* (Glasgow, 1969)

Spufford, M., *The Great Reclothing of Rural England. Petty Chapmen and their Wares in the Seventeenth Century* (1984)

Walsham, A., *Providence in Early Modern England* (Oxford, 1999)

Watt, T., *Cheap Print and Popular Piety, 1550–1640* (Cambridge, 1993)

Weatherill, L., *Consumer Behaviour and Material Culture in Britain, 1660–1760* (1988)

Williams, P., *The Later Tudors. England, 1547–1603* (Oxford, 1995)

Wrightson, K., *Earthly Necessities. Economic Lives in Early Modern Britain* (2000)

2. Style

Baarsen, R., Jackson-Stops, G., Johnston, P. M. and Dee, E., *Courts and Colonies. The William and Mary Style in Holland, England and America* (1988)

Harris, J. and Higgott, G., *Inigo Jones. Complete Architectural Drawings* (1989)

Harris, J., Orgel, S. and Strong, R. (eds), *The King's Arcadia: Inigo Jones and the Stuart Court* (1973)

Honour, H., *Chinoiserie: The Vision of Cathay* (1961)

Impey, O., *Chinoiserie: The Impact of Oriental Styles on Western Art and Decoration* (1977)

Mowl, T., *Elizabethan and Jacobean Style* (1993)

Peacock, J., *The Stage Designs of Inigo Jones. The European Context* (Cambridge, 1995)

Summerson, J. N., *Architecture in Britain, 1530–1830* (1991)

Summerson, J. N., *Inigo Jones* (1966)

Ward Jackson, P. W., *Some Mainstreams and Tributaries in European Ornament from 1500 to 1750* (1967)

Wells-Cole, A., *Art and Decoration in Elizabethan and Jacobean England: The Influence of Continental Prints, 1558–1625* (1997)

3. Who led taste?

Anglo, S., (ed.), *Chivalry in the Renaissance* (Woodbridge, 1990)

Anglo, S., *Spectacle, Pageantry, and Early Tudor Policy* (Oxford, 1969)

Brown, J., *Kings and Connoisseurs: Collecting Art in Seventeenth-Century Europe* (Princeton, NJ, 1995)

Bucholz, R. O., *The Augustan Court: Queen Anne and the Decline of Court Culture* (Stanford, CA, 1993)

Dunlop, I., *Palaces and Progresses of Elizabeth I* (1962)

Gent, L., *Albion's Classicism: The Visual Arts in England, 1550–1650* (1995)

Girouard, M., *Robert Smythson and the Elizabethan Country House* (1983)

Griffiths, A., *The Print in Stuart Britain, 1603–1689* (1998)

Gunn, S. J. and Lindley, P. G., *Cardinal Wolsey. Church, State and Art* (Cambridge, 1991)

Harris, E., *British Architectural Books and Writers, 1556–1785* (Cambridge, 1990)

Harris, J., *The Artist and the Country House. A History of Country House and Garden View Painting in Britain, 1540–1870* (1979)

Howarth, D. (ed.), *Art and Patronage in the Caroline Courts* (Cambridge, 1993)

Howarth, D., *Images of Rule. Art and Politics in the English Renaissance, 1485–1649* (1997)

Howarth, D., *Lord Arundel and his Circle* (1985)

Jervis, S., *The Penguin Dictionary of Design and Designers* (1984)

Jervis, S., *Printed Furniture Designs before 1650* (1974)

Lytle, G. F. and Orgel, S. (eds), *Patronage in the Renaissance* (Princeton, NJ, 1982)

Maccubbin, R. P. and Hamilton-Phillips, M., *The Age of William III and Mary II: Power, Politics and Patronage, 1688–1702* (Williamsburg, VA, 1989)

Maclean, G., *Culture and Society in the Stuart Restoration: Literature, Drama, History* (Cambridge, 1995)

Murdoch, T., *Boughton House. The English Versailles* (1992)

O'Connell, S., *The Popular Print in England: 1550–1850* (1999)

Orgel, S., *The Illusion of Power: Political Theater in the English Renaissance* (Berkeley, CA, 1975)

Parry, G., *The Golden Age Restor'd. The Culture of the Stuart Court, 1603–42* (1981)

Peck, L. L., *Court, Patronage and Corruption in Early Stuart England* (Boston, MA, 1990)

Sharpe, K., *The Personal Rule of Charles I* (1992)

Starkey, D. (ed.), *Henry VIII, A European Court in England* (1991)

Strong, R. C., *The Cult of Elizabeth: Elizabethan Portraiture and Pagentry* (1977)

Strong, R. C., *Splendour at Court: Renaissance Spectacle and Illusion* (1973)

Thurley, S., *The Royal Palaces of Tudor England: Architecture and Court Life, 1460–1547* (1993)

Veevers, E., *Images of Love and Religion. Queen Henrietta and Court Entertainments* (Cambridge, 1989)

4. Fashionable living

Airs, M., *The Tudor and Jacobean Country House. A Building History* (1995)

Arnold, J., *Queen Elizabeth's Wardrobe Unlock'd* (Leeds, 1988)

Arthur, L., *Embroidery 1600–1700 at the Burrell Collection* (1995)

Ashelford, J., *The Art of Dress. Clothes and Society, 1500–1914* (1996)

Ashelford, J., *Dress in the Age of Elizabeth I* (1988)

Barry, J. (ed.), *The Tudor and Stuart Town, 1530–1688. A Reader in English Urban History* (1990)

Cliffe, J. T., *The World of the Country House in Seventeenth-Century England* (1999)

Cooper, N., *Houses of the Gentry, 1480–1680* (1999)

Cox, N., *The Complete Tradesman: A Study of Retailing, 1550–1820* (Aldershot, 2000)

Croft-Murray, E., *Decorative Painting in England 1537–1837. Vol. 1. Early Tudor to Sir James Thornhill* (1962)

Cumming, V., *A Visual History of Costume: The Seventeenth Century* (1984)

Friedman, A. T., *House and Household in Elizabethan England: Wollaton Hall and the Willoughby Family* (Chicago, IL, 1989)

Girouard, M., *Life in the English Country House: A Social and Architectural History* (1978)

Heal, F. and Holmes, C., *The Gentry in England and Wales, 1500–1700* (1994)

Hearn, K. (ed.), *Dynasties: Painting in Tudor and Jacobean England, 1530–1630* (1995)

Holmes, M., *Elizabethan London* (1969)

Howard, M., *The Early Tudor Country House. Architecture and Politics, 1490–1550* (1987)

Hunt, J. D., *Garden and Grove. The Italian Renaissance Garden and the English Imagination, 1600–1750* (1986)

Jackson-Stops, G. (ed.), *The Fashioning and Functioning of the British Country House* (Washington, DC, 1989)

King, D. and Levey, S. M., *The Victoria and Albert Museum's Textile Collection: Embroidery in Britain from 1200 to 1750* (1993)

Lawrence, A., *Women in England, 1500–1760: A Social History* (1994)

Levey, S. M., *An Elizabethan Inheritance: The Hardwick Hall Textiles* (1998)

Lewellyn, N., *The Art of Death: Visual Culture in the English Death Ritual, c. 1500–c. 1800* (1991)

Mendelson, S. and Crawford, P., *Women in Early Modern England 1550–1720* (Oxford, 1998)

Mercer, E., *English Art, 1553–1625* (Oxford, 1962)

Mertes, K., *The English Noble Household, 1260–1600: Good Governance and Political Rule* (Oxford, 1988)

Platt, C., *The Architecture of Medieval Britain: A Social History* (1990)

Platt, C., *The Great Rebuildings of Tudor and Stuart England: Revolutions in Architectural Taste* (1994)

Schofield, J., *The Building of London: from the Conquest to the Great Fire* (1984)

Strong, R. C., *The Artist and the Garden* (2000)

Strong, R. C., *The Tudor and Stuart Monarchy: Pageantry, Painting, Iconography* (3 vols, Woodbridge, 1995–8)

Thornton, P. K., *Seventeenth-Century Interior Decoration in England, France and Holland* (1978)

Wyman, S. E., *Sociability and Power in Late-Stuart England. The Cultural Worlds of the Verneys, 1660–1720* (Oxford, 1999)

5. What was new?

Archer, M., *Delftware: The Tin-Glazed Earthenware of the British Isles* (1997)

Blake, N. F., *Caxton, England's First Publisher* (1976)

Charleston, R. J., *English Glass and the Glass used in England, c. 400–1940* (1984)

Chaudhuri, K. N., *The Trading World of Asia and the English East India Company, 1660–1760* (Cambridge, 1978)

Feather, J., *A History of British Publishing* (1988)

Gaimster, D., *German Stoneware 1200–1900* (1997)

Glanville, P., *Silver in Tudor and Early Stuart England* (1990)

Godfrey, E. S., *The Development of English Glass Making, 1560–1640* (Oxford, 1975)

Goodman, J., *Tobacco in History: The Cultures of Dependence* (1993)

Goodman, J., Lovejoy, P. E. and Sherratt, A. (eds), *Consuming Habits: Drugs in History and Anthropology* (1995)

Green, C., *John Dwight's Fulham Pottery* (1999)

Harris, J., *Essays in Industry and Technology in the Eighteenth Century: England and France* (Hampshire, 1992)

Harte, N.B. (ed.), *The New Draperies in the Low Countries and England, 1300–1800* (Oxford, 1997)

Hatcher, J. and Barker, T. C., *A History of British Pewter* (1974)

Hellinga, L. and Trapp, J. B. (eds), *The Cambridge History of the Book in Britain, Vol. 3, 1400–1557* (Cambridge, 1999)

Hodnett, E., *Five Centuries of English Book Illustration* (Aldershot, 1988)

Hunter, M., *Science and Society in Restoration England* (Cambridge, 1981)

Irwin, J., 'Origins of the "Oriental Style" in English Decorative Art', *Burlington Magazine*, 97 (1955)

Irwin, J. and Brett, K. B., *Origins of Chintz* (1970)

Lavery, B., *The Ship of the Line* (1983)

Loomes, B., *The Early Clockmakers of Great Britain* (1981)

Mitchell, D., *Goldsmiths, Silversmiths and Bankers. Innovation and the Transfer of Skill, 1550 to 1750* (1995)

North, A., *Pewter at the Victoria and Albert Museum* (1999)

Roger, N. A. M., *The Safeguard of the Sea: A Naval History of Britain: Vol. 1. 660–1649* (1997)

Rothstein, N., *The Victoria and Albert Museum's Textile Collection. Woven Textile Design in Britain to 1750* (1994)

Smith, M. M., *The Title-Page. Its Early Development, 1460–1510* (2000)

Styles, J., 'Product Innovation in Early-Modern London', *Past and Present*, 168 (2000)

Sutherland, J., *The Restoration Newspaper and its Development* (Cambridge, 1986)

Thirsk, J., *Economic Policy and Projects. The Development of a Consumer Society in Early Modern England* (Oxford, 1978)

V&A Museum, *The Needle's Excellency: A Travelling Exhibition* (1973)

Picture Credits

Index